# GREAT AMERICAN
# THOROUGHBRED
# RACETRACKS

# GREAT AMERICAN
# THOROUGHBRED
# RACETRACKS

Photographs and Text by Nancy Stout

Foreword by Eddie Arcaro

RIZZOLI
NEW YORK

First published in the United States of America in 1991 by
RIZZOLI INTERNATIONAL PUBLICATIONS, INC.
300 Park Avenue South, New York, NY 10010

This project was supported in part by a grant from the National Endowment for
the Arts, a Federal Agency.

Library of Congress Cataloging-in-Publication Data
Stout, Nancy
Great American Thoroughbred Racetracks/photographs and text by
Nancy Stout: foreword by Eddie Arcaro.
p.   cm.
Includes bibliographical references (p.   ) and index.
ISBN 0-8478-1382-7
1. Racetracks (Horse-racing)—United States—History. 2. Horse-racing—United
States—History.  3. Thoroughbred horse—United States—History.  I. Title.
SF324..3.S76  1991          91-4484
798.4'006'873—dc20          CIP

Design by Charles Davey
Printed and bound by la cromolito, Milan, Italy
Jacket: Churchill Downs, Louisville, Kentucky
Photograph of Eddie Arcaro by Jerry Cooke

# CONTENTS

# ACKNOWLEDGMENTS

Certain people helped enormously with this project. Carole Bergman, Winston Kulok, William Pollak, and others donated money so that I could work on the book. Ron Warren read the manuscript, made suggestions, and asked questions. Jerry Cooke and James Bassett were generous with information and sometimes acted as troubleshooters. Cathy Schenck, Librarian at Keeneland, helped assemble primary sources for the text and provided the bibliography. Racing writer Joe Hirsch gave his interest and support. Bob Curran, *Thoroughbred Racing Communications*, helped in many ways. David Morton, my editor at Rizzoli, made writing the book a little easier with his kind encouragement. Lexington Labs printed the pictures with care and enthusiasm. Stan Scottland kindly accepted my absence from work while I traveled throughout the country. The staff of the American Film Institute searched for racing films in their cataloguing project and the U.C.L.A. Film Archives assisted me in viewing them.

I'd also like to thank the many people who assisted me with the individual racetracks. **Arlington:** Larry Oltmanns, Skidmore, Owings & Merrill; Neil Milbert, racing columnist, *The Chicago Tribune*; Tim Samuelson, Commission on Chicago Landmarks; **Belmont:** Tom Durkin and Trevor Denman, track announcers; Leonard Goodman, agent; architects Robert Krause and John Manley; Pedro Villanueva, John Olin, and Andy Dudley, New York Racing Association. **Churchill Downs:** James H. Charleton, Historian, National Park Service; Marty Perry, Kentucky Heritage Council; Jim Bolus; Randy Ray, Director, Kentucky Derby Museum. **Del Mar:** Bruce Kamerling, San Diego Historical Society; Mary Allely, San Diego Public Library; Morio Kow, Froehlich, Kow & Gong; Larry Guthrie, California State Architect's Office. **Fair Grounds:** John Ferguson, New Orleans Historic District Landmarks Commission; Sandra Salmen and Louie Roussel III. **Gulfstream:** David Lair, Steward, Steward & Skinner; Jose M. Lozano; Douglas Donn. **Hialeah:** John Brunetti, Lester Geisler. **Keeneland:** Charles Graves, School of Architecture, University of Kentucky; James Williams; Sandra Hamilton; Morio Kow, Froehlich, Kow & Gong; Jim Bolus. **Monmouth:** L. Rex Anderson, Linenthal, Eisenberg, Anderson, Inc.; Mrs. Philip H. Iselin. **Oaklawn:** Charles Cella; Lee Brandsford, Engineering Consultants, Little Rock, Arkansas; Don Grisham, *Daily Racing Form*. **Santa Anita:** David Gebhard, Robert Strub, Gwynn Wilson, Jane Goldstein, James Kilroe, William Adler. **Saratoga:** Mark Costello, Sam Kanchuger, Michael Veitch, Kenneth Reynolds, Jr., John Brownrigg; David Zdunczyk, Director, National Museum of Racing and Hall of Fame; Dr. Martha Stonequist.

# FOREWORD

I know as much about architecture as Frank Lloyd Wright knew about the daily double. But I've jockeyed at over one hundred racetracks in the United States and Canada, and at others in Europe and Australia, and I always take the time to look around and view the local scenery. Each track has its own distinct character and spirit, and whether you're a jockey, a spectator, or even a Thoroughbred, the spirit of the place is always with you.

I'm not an architecture critic, but I know what I like. I've always thought that Hialeah in Miami and Santa Anita near Los Angeles are the most beautiful tracks I've seen, at least in this part of the world. Both tracks impress one with their great natural beauty—Hialeah with its lush vegetation and royal palm trees, and Santa Anita with its matchless backdrop of the San Gabriel mountains. Neither track is new, but both are as smart and elegant in appearance today as they were when they were built. But even without these beautiful settings, Hialeah and Santa Anita would stand out for the quality all horsemen seek in Thoroughbreds of exceptional ability—that quality called class.

The history of the tracks themselves and my own experiences in riding at them have a strong bearing on how I feel about them. But I get a special sensation at Hialeah and Santa Anita that I don't get at other tracks. It's a good feeling—part excitement, part anticipation, part admiration, part serenity. It's easy to ride at these tracks and always enjoyable. That is probably the ultimate compliment a laymen like myself can pay to an architect.

In my thirty years as a jockey, my favorite track has always been Belmont Park in New York, principally because of its size. It's the largest track in the United States at a mile-and-a-half in circumference, and the best horse usually has the best chance to win on a large track. I have been fortunate enough to be on the best horse in many races throughout my career and I've always wanted the room to maneuver. Belmont, with its sweeping turns and galloping stretches, offers plenty of room.

If I were a casual fan, however, who came to the races once a week and wanted a good view of the horses and as much comfort as possible, I'd probably pick the new Arlington International Racecourse in Chicago. Because it opened in 1989, it incorporates many state-of-the-art facilities for the comfort of the public. You can see the horses from every seat; you get a confirmation from overhead television; and the architecture is light and uplifting to the spirit. Particular credit is due the track's chairman, Dick Duchossois, who insisted on good sightlines and a lively building style.

If a day of fun at the races were my goal, there are three tracks with the ambience and classic spirit for such an outing: Saratoga Race Course, in Saratoga Springs, New York; Oaklawn Park in Hot Springs, Arkansas; and Keeneland Race Course in Lexington,

Kentucky. Saratoga is rustic. Oaklawn Park is fine for a family outing. And Keeneland hosts a racing community among the most knowledgeable and sophisticated in the country. Their common denominator is an atmosphere of informality and charm—rare qualities in any environment—and the crowds invariably leave in good spirits, whether they've won or lost.

A special word about Churchill Downs, where I rode my five Kentucky Derby winners: it has more atmosphere than any other track in this country. You just look at it and your mind drifts back to some of the great horses and great Derbies of the past: Whirlaway, with his long tail flapping behind him as he wins by eight lengths; Native Dancer, roughed at the first turn and beaten by a head by Dark Star, the only loss of his career; and Seattle Slew, bursting between horses after a moderate start and charging to a lead he never relinquished. The rambling Churchill Downs stands look like they were put together by a committee, but somehow they capture the spirit and tradition of the Run for the Roses, America's greatest race. And if you're lucky enough to be sitting on one of the starters when they come out onto the track and the band plays "My Old Kentucky Home" and you hear 100,000 spectators join in with "Weep no more my lady . . . ," you get a jolt in the heart, whether you're riding in your first or your twenty-first—and that comes from personal experience.

Architecture can affect our outlook on the world in many ways, at work, at home, or at play. For this reason Nancy Stout's work interested me from the start. Through her photographs and her writings I learned much about America's racetracks that I never knew before, despite my many years among them. If you enjoy this work half as much as I have, you cannot fail to take a good, long look around the next time you visit a racetrack. You may be, as I have time and again, pleasantly surprised.

*Eddie Arcaro*
*Miami, 1991*

# INTRODUCTION

This book profiles twelve of the finest American Thoroughbred racetracks. It is about buildings and people—a history of the architects and clients of these facilities, how they were financed, how they have changed over the years, and, more significantly, how Thoroughbred racing has been Americanized. The photographs document all the parts of each racetrack, and in some instances include private clubrooms and stable areas that are normally restricted. Almost no horses are mentioned because the task at hand is to describe the places themselves.

The racetracks treated herein are the following: Saratoga Race Course, located in Saratoga Springs, New York, which opened in 1864; the Fair Grounds in New Orleans, the third-oldest American track and the lone survivor of racing in the South, established in 1872; Oaklawn Park, located in Hot Springs, Arkansas, built in 1902; Belmont Park, a survivor of New York City's many racetracks, established in 1905; three beautiful racing facilities built after parimutuel wagering was legalized in the Depression—Hialeah Park in Miami, Santa Anita Park in Los Angeles, and Del Mar Fairgrounds north of San Diego; two Kentucky tracks, Churchill Downs in Louisville, built in 1872 to revive the Thoroughbred industry after the Civil War, and Keeneland Race Course in Lexington, established in 1936 to showcase the state's most important commodity, Kentucky-bred Thoroughbreds; Monmouth Park, on the Jersey shore, and Gulfstream, located in Miami, built in the 1940s as resort tracks; and, finally, one of the newest racing facilities, Arlington International Racecourse near Chicago, built in 1989 to replace an older facility destroyed by fire. Each track hosts premier racing.

The old resort tracks located at watering places—Saratoga and Oaklawn—started as small, beautifully designed racetracks and developed into greatly expanded facilities, yet they both retain a rustic quality and sense of romance. The newer racetracks, built in the 1930s after years of a weak economy and a strong public sentiment against racing, were designed to be substantial but glamorous; the best examples of this are Hialeah's French Revival architecture and tropical gardens, and Santa Anita's Neo-Georgian clubhouse and streamlined grandstand. Keeneland, also a product of the 1930s, reflects a conservatism and pride in the tradition of early agricultural fairs, and is a country estate adapted for re-use as a racetrack. The old track at Belmont, built in 1905, is also a former country estate; its best man-made features, however, are not the buildings but the grand racing course and the overall landscaping. The magnificent balance of art and engineering at Belmont makes this track the ideal forum for a discussion of the history of racing as well as racetrack architecture.

The Thoroughbred is a racing horse whose pedigree has been developed for about 250 years. Although its origin is English, the breeding and racing history of the Thoroughbred is concurrent with the development of American racing facilities, which evolved in a manner quite unlike those in Europe. Our history and character intervened. Pragmatically, Americans chose to race in an oval rather than in a straight line, and on dirt instead of grass, choices that in 1665 may have seemed arbitrary, but were continued for monetary reasons. Furthermore, we run horses early, at the age of two, on shortened distances, because most of our oval tracks are one mile in circumference and are, compared to the English racing strips, shortened tracks. Finally, we have taken a day at the races and turned it into a hefty business venture between the racetrack and the state, which encourages and depends upon the income generated by daily betting.

Thoroughbreds were brought to America in two phases. They arrived with English settlers in the seventeenth and eighteenth centuries and were raced and bred wherever settlements were established—New York, Maryland, Virginia, Kentucky, and South Carolina, in particular. The old racetracks and stud farms of the south did not survive the Civil War, and only in Kentucky, which was neutral, did the bloodlines survive and flourish. The second phase seems to have come when A.B. Hancock of Claiborne Farm in Lexington, Kentucky, purchased English horses of superior quality, with either good stud records or good racing records (Sir Galahad III was purchased in 1925 and Blenheim II in 1936), and brought them to Kentucky to stand at his farm. In 1950 A.B. "Bull" Hancock, Jr. purchased Nasrullah, the great horse bred by the Aga Khan, for Claiborne Farm. The major stallions currently standing and successful on racetracks throughout the world can be traced back to Northern Dancer, sired by Neartic, or Bold Ruler, sired by Nasrullah.

This project began with a grant from the Design Arts Program of the National Endowment for the Arts to document the architecture, landscape design, and historic preservation of the major American Thoroughbred racetracks. The original project included only six tracks—Belmont, Hialeah, Keeneland, Oaklawn, Saratoga, and Santa Anita. These were chosen because of their longevity, importance to racing (Grade I, II, and III races), and architectural integrity (it is for this reason that Pimlico, the nation's second oldest racetrack, now extremely altered, was eliminated). In 1988 I began to catalogue the elements that comprise a racetrack: grandstand, clubhouse, dirt and turf courses, infield, paddock, walking circle, horse path or gap, barns, training tracks, backstretch kitchens, entrance gates, parking lots, graphics, souvenir stands, landscape architecture, and garden furniture. I tried to discover who built these facilities, how much they cost, who the architect was, and how much of the initial design has been preserved and how much has been modified. This is a photographic document of these racetracks as they currently appear.

# GREAT AMERICAN THOROUGHBRED RACETRACKS

# ARLINGTON INTERNATIONAL RACECOURSE

## ARLINGTON HEIGHTS, ILLINOIS

Erected in 1927 and made of steel and glass, Arlington Park was the first great modern racing facility. The racetrack at Arlington Park had been organized by H.D. "Curley" Brown, who built, managed, and renovated racetracks. According to the American Racing Manual, his projects included: in 1890, a track called Clear Lodge in Montana; in 1909, one in Moncreif Park, Jacksonville, Florida; in 1911, Laurel Park in Maryland; in 1912, a track in Charleston, South Carolina; and in 1915, Oriental Park, Havana, Cuba. His backers for the Arlington project were Laurance Armour, Armour & Company; John Hertz, Yellow Cab Co.; Weymouth Kirkland, lawyer; Otto Lehman, retailer; Major Frederick McLaughlin, owner of the Chicago Blackhawks; and John R. Thompson, owner of Thompson's Restaurant. They purchased 1,000 acres of productive crop land for over one million dollars and constructed a track with grandstand seating for 16,000, a railway station, stables for up to 2,700 horses, and a track with two racing ovals, one of dirt and an inner turf track. They developed tennis courts and a polo field, among other facilities, making this an early sports complex. The entire facility is estimated to have cost about two million dollars, largely because of the enormous acreage of productive farmland purchased at pre-stock-market-crash prices.

The new racing facility at Arlington was built by owner Richard L. Duchossois after the existing racetrack burned in 1985. His brilliance seems to be that he has recognized the fact that, these days, far fewer people go to the racetrack, and he has tried to create a new market by creating a facility that is as much for spectator sports as it is for gambling. And, although Arlington has always been a vanguard racetrack in its embrace of turf racing, he has made it a pursuit, renaming the track Arlington International Racecourse and establishing a bonus system to encourage horses from Longchamps, in Paris, to run there. Duchossois hopes to make Arlington a neutral racing ground where horses from Europe can compete with California and New York horses.

15

*Left:* Owner's apartment in the grandstand *Overleaf:* The grandstand

The new grandstand and paddock area at Arlington opened in 1989 (Skidmore, Owings & Merrill, Chicago, architects; McHugh Construction Company, general contractors), to the surprise and delight of most people in the racing world. The grandstand is tiny, measuring 680 by 150 feet, and can be compared in size to the oldest portion of the wooden grandstand at Saratoga, built in 1892 (approximately 585 by 250 feet). The new facility is half the length of the present grandstands at both Saratoga and Belmont Park, which were expanded to accommodate racing attendance when it peaked in the 1960s.

The new facilities at Arlington also represent a return to the traditional, exposed, single-tier stand. In general, modern racetrack grandstands are stacked tiers totally enclosed by glass on the side facing the track, seating many patrons over the finish line (the best example of this is Garden State Park, Ewing Cole Parsky Cherry, Philadelphia; Robert Krause, design architect). The new Arlington stand turns this concept around, stacking patrons over the paddock but allowing them balconies, fresh air, proximity to the horses, and a glass wall. The front facing the track has open seating unencumbered by glass walls for its entire length, and with two upper tiers, set well back and enclosed, contains a restaurant and the Turf Club, which is designed to curve outward in order to improve the visibility down the homestretch. Corporate boxes are located just under the roof, along an open balcony.

The building is exceptionally narrow, keeping the focus on what is happening outside. In the center of each floor is an electronic communications system displaying betting-related statistics on a long, black-glass screen. There are no TV lounges; for people who cannot tolerate natural light and fresh air, a separate building is located on the other side of the racetrack. It is dark, smoke-filled, and dotted with TV monitors.

The paddock runs the full length of the grandstand and is sloped down at the center to allow good views of the walking circle. There are balconies on every floor of the back of the grandstand to encourage interest in the activities taking place in the paddock. It is enclosed on all sides by buildings: the clubhouse and grandstand entrance gatehouses are at the ends; the saddling shed is in the center and is flanked by the jockeys' quarters and the maintenance offices.

The most important innovation of the track is clearly the sunken paddock. It is designed to be the center of all activity between the races and is easily accessible to every patron who cares to take a short walk to the back of the building. It occupies the full length of the back of the grandstand building and was inspired in part by Gulfstream, which has a centrally located axis running from the saddling shed through the oval walking ring, directly through the center of the building and out onto the track. But whereas Gulfstream is a flat space, Arlington is sunken—creating a better view. The effect is much more theatrical but the patrons do not have the benefit of being close to the horses, which is still possible at Santa Anita. Keeneland, with its long *allée* running the full length of the building, primarily for the benefit of the grandstand patrons, is another example of a paddock as the center of all activity. The location of the paddock at Belmont and Monmouth is primarily for the benefit of the clubhouse area.

The scale has been manipulated at the back of the building so that it does not appear too

*Above*: Horse path to the paddock through the saddling shed

*Below:* The paddock

tall for the shallow paddock. The roof slopes downward to reduce the scale of the glass wall by one story at the top. Likewise, the ground level is raised at the edge of the building to reduce the visual height yet another story. This puts everything that is on the ground level really in the basement, and on the other side of the building, the apron is graded one full story from the edge of the building to the edge of the track. This landscape engineering, which turns six stories into four, hides the entire floor of administration offices and makes viewing anywhere from the apron excellent. The grandstand's appearance of being long and low, with its emphasis on horizontal lines, makes it sympathetic to its setting on the prairie. Emphasis of the roof, making it look bigger, is an old trick favored by Chicago architects.

The "cultural construction" that was attempted as a means of linking Arlington to the world of racing through the use of distinctive materials has not been an unmitigated success. There is a variety of heavy timbers and slate shingles, painted bricks, steeples, bronze weather vanes, and pink brick pavement mixed with glass curtain walls and aluminum in an

*Above:* Clubhouse grandstand and terrace

effort to make the new Arlington look traditional. "This constant contrast of the modern with the historic creates a unique identity and makes connections with racing traditions, while establishing Arlington Park as a state-of-the-art facility of the twenty-first century," explains Larry Oltmanns of Skidmore, Owings & Merrill. One of the ways this was attempted was by copying the shape of the steel trusses on the enclosure, creating a sort of bargeboard. This seems to be an excessive detail, simply part of an alphabet of architectural ornament that is applied to all parts of the racetrack, inside and out, when all it takes is one element, such as Keeneland's stone arches, Hialeah's flamingos, Oaklawn's mountain air, or Saratoga's wooden chairs and relentless summer heat, to form a strong identity.

*Above:* Turf Club dinnerware

*Below:* The Turf Club bar

*Overleaf:* Infield tote board

MIN. TO POST

*Above:* Widener Turf Course from the clubhouse

# BELMONT PARK

There are three elements that distinguish the Americanization of Thoroughbred racing: the races are run on an oval track, usually one mile in length; they are run on a dirt surface; and turf courses are located within the oval dirt track. In England, the motherland of racing, races are run on a straight or irregular course that is guided by the terrain. Racing fans make no attempt to see the entire race, as they do in America, because the courses are vast; their first races were run in royal parks where there was ample room. In the English colonies— Africa, Australia, and India, for example—the courses are large and follow the English prototype. Furthermore, throughout the rest of the world, except for a few places in South America, all races are run on grass.

Our American fathers, who began racing in 1665 in Hempstead, Long Island, ran their horses on a course two miles around because of the difficulty of clearing the dense forests. By the eighteenth century, races were regularly conducted on oval courses all over America, usually a mile in circumference, and they were run counterclockwise on the dirt. The oval is revolutionary primarily because it introduces the new element of turns and, assuming that the oval is small enough, it allows racing fans to see the entire race. A dirt track provides a harder, faster surface and is durable enough to be used in all weather and every day; grass, however, is fragile and must be used selectively.

There are several explanations for the choice of Americans to run their horses on dirt. It is faster and can be run on every day. However, the main reason involves the enormous amount of money racing generates. A dirt track allows many races to be run in a day, every day, even though it is hard on the horses. Our priorities are clearly divergent with those of the racing countries of Europe, where the racetracks are located within the same area, and racing is alternated from one track to another for about three days at each in order to preserve the turf and the horses. Trevor Denham, Santa Anita's race commentator, noted that "That is why the English, the Irish, and the French will never build dirt tracks, which are too hard on the horses. In a perfect world we would run on turf and would alternate racetracks. We would run on turf for the benefit of the horses, and we would alternate racetracks for the benefit of the turf. And if the American system was the ultimate system, then, believe me, those other countries would adopt it because they would love to race every day. Obviously, they would love to be financially better off."

American turf courses were added after the dirt tracks were built and are therefore within the oval. Many have been added in the last decade as grass racing has gained in popularity. Tom Durkin, Belmont Park's race caller, says, "Every racetrack would race on grass if they could. People bet more money on grass races, grass is more aesthetically pleasing, and truer races are run on grass when the circumstances are right. Horses prefer it because it is easier on their legs, so trainers prefer, in many cases, to run their horses on grass. The only problem is that we run races every day at American racetracks, but the wear and tear on grass is such that you just can't do it every day. In Europe they run a couple of days in the spring and perhaps four days in the fall, so you can run on the grass. Here we run sixty races a week for four or five months, so it is impossible."

The main dirt track at Belmont Park, built in 1905, is the largest course in America. It is considered by many to be the country's best course because it is the biggest, measuring 1½ miles around, and because it has wide turns. Durkin, who is one of perhaps fifty people in the world whose job it is to observe a race in motion and call the position of the horses, says that, "Belmont was designed for classic races, and the truest races are run here because of the size of the racetrack, but it is hard for fans to see the race."

Classic races are a set of races for three-year-old horses, of fixed distances and run on the same days every year. The most famous classic races in America are the Kentucky Derby, with a distance of 1¼ miles, the Preakness at 1³⁄₁₆ miles, and the Belmont Stakes at 1½ miles. The Derby is run on the first Saturday in May, the Preakness two weeks later, and the final race at Belmont Park three weeks after the Preakness, in mid-June. These three together are called the Triple Crown and determine our national champion Thoroughbreds. The truest races are those with as little as possible left to chance. Newmarket, in England, is a straight course and the truest race of all, but the truest American race is at Belmont because of the substantial distance between the turns and the width of the turns themselves. Durkin notes that "In Europe you run from here to there—that is really the truest race, but here you have to run around two turns, and here to there is longer for the horses who have to race on the outside of the turns." In other words, the jockey must quickly position the horse next to the rail on entering the turns.

According to Trevor Denman, "Horses that have an outside post have to run faster to get into a good position. When you are going into the first turn you have to run faster, consuming more energy, which means you've got less left later. You don't necessarily have to run farther because you start off in a straight line. All it means is drifting over a little—you might lose a fraction of ground, but you have to run faster to clear the other horses so you can reach the inside rail. If you can't run fast enough you will lose ground because you will have to run three or four horses wide. Or you have to be a come-from-behind horse, not care about your post position, and just drop in last."

According to Durkin, "At Belmont, in the 1½-mile race here, the horses have a longer distance to run before entering the first turn, so there are all sorts of opportunities to get to the inside, go to the outside, and place the horse where it is most comfortable running. Also, the races where you have to go into a sharp turn are much more dangerous, and jockeys must run much more carefully. When you have ten horses who want to save ground and get on the inside in a very cramped space, it's a lot more difficult than when you have a

*Right:* Road from the barn area to the clubhouse

*Above:* View of the Widener Turf Course, the Inner Turf Course, a steeplechase course, and the infield lake

great expanse to run in."

This problem is solved by building an appendage, called a chute, onto the track. In Thoroughbred racing the total distance is marked by furlongs, or ⅛-mile intervals, from the finish line back to the start. The usual distance for Thoroughbreds to race is at least six furlongs, but the six-furlong pole is on the first turn—not a good place to start. Therefore, a chute, or an extra length of track, is added, permitting the race to end on the finish line and not start on the turn. This makes a truer race and retains our faith in the oval track. It is a concession to American racing history and the beauty of the oval, as well as our general greediness to see it all. And these are some of the problems: for example, if it is a one-mile race on a one-mile track, is a true race one in which the start is also on the finish line or should the start be at a chute? Some racetracks even move the finish line. At Keeneland, for example, the finish line is moved up the track, which places it in front of the clubhouse. According to Durkin, this is not a true race because there is not a long stretch to the finish, which is good for some horses, although he admits that the 1¹⁄₁₆-mile oval at Keeneland "is just about right. Not too big, not too small, cozier."

There are really three track sizes: Belmont is the largest at 1½ miles, many of the major tracks such as Aqueduct and Arlington are 1⅛ miles, Keeneland is an oddity at 1¹⁄₁₆ miles, and Santa Anita and Churchill Downs have courses measuring one mile. Belmont Park track

*Above:* The grandstand

superintendent Joe King says that the main track was changed in the 1950s, "pulled in" to create a bus road at the edge of the track, but in 1960–61 it was restored to a full 1½-mile oval. Likewise, a diagonal chute across the infield, known as the Widener chute, was eliminated and the name was given to the outer turf track. Two engineering firms have worked on the tracks, Lockwood & Kessler and Andrews & Clark.

There are two turf tracks at Belmont, a feature unique to this racetrack. Aqueduct also once had a main track and two turf courses, but in 1975–76 the outer turf track was changed to dirt to make a track suitable for winter racing. These two New York tracks are the only ones in the country with three courses. Arlington had two turf tracks, but converted them into a wider single track. Belmont's two turf courses measure 1³⁄₁₆ and 1¹⁄₁₆ miles, and are also of substantial width. By moving the "dogs," or railings, three to six feet, which can be done due to the exceptional width of the turf courses, there can be a reduction of wear and tear on any one section of the grass. This means that grass races can be run every day of the season by alternating the course used and, with good maintenance and proper irrigation, the grass can be sustained. Of course, much depends on the weather, because races run in the rain damage the turf.

The infield at Belmont is a cleanly landscaped area with centrally located lakes. These lakes, which are found in many infields, seem to be used primarily as a means to reduce grounds maintenance, eliminating the need to cut perhaps a hundred acres of grass. The Belmont infield, because of the lake, is a landing spot on the migration route for Canadian geese; hundreds flock there and can be seen during The Jockey Club Gold Cup held the first Saturday in October. There are always sea gulls from the nearby coast, but they occasionally spook the horses, and so are not particularly welcome.

The Belmont Park backside, or stable area, more than at any other track, resembles a small rural town. Approximately 800 people live there year-round in eighty cottages. In addition to the horses owned by outside shippers who bring their horses in for particular races, 2,300 horses are stabled there. There are sixty-two barns and sixty-seven outbuildings, as well as garages, maintenance shops, greenhouses, and two restaurants, which are always referred to at racetracks as "kitchens." The keepers of the property are the Resident Manager and the Assistant Resident Manager, Alan Mehldau and John Olin, who maintain the buildings, roads, and landscaping. There are tree-lined streets named after famous

*Above:* Racing depicted in ironwork

horses, although this was done fairly recently: Man O'War, Count Fleet, Citation, and Secretariat are horse paths and dirt tracks that have been in use for nearly a century. All electric and gas lines are buried, contributing to the area's timeless look.

The earliest barns were constructed within twenty or thirty years after the track was built. The Whitney, Mellon, and Phipps families constructed three of the barns, which have been used by their stables ever since. Built at the owners' expense, the early barns are long shed rows composed of a series of stalls, usually measuring ten by twelve feet, with a shed roof covering a walking track. They are built of wood with slate roofs and are painted dark green; subsequent barns, now of cement block, are compatible in style. Many of the barns

*Above:* Steeplechase depicted on iron fence overlooking the walking circle

*Below:* Stable hand with horse depicted on ironwork

have adjacent cottages or two-story frame houses, which were built to provide offices and living rooms on the ground floor for the trainers and rooms upstairs for their staff. Although the cottages are still used by hot walkers and grooms, the trainers rarely keep offices there. Only two, Woody Stephens and Bill Hirsch, keep these old facilities as a kind of memento. Two of the most attractive barns are pairs of shed rows joined to make elliptically shaped structures now called the "round barns." One pair of these adjoined barns is used by Rokeby Stable and Mackenzie Miller, trainer for Paul Mellon. Mellon's father built the barns approximately eighty-five years ago, and they were connected in the 1920s by curved cement-block structures. This ellipse forms an indoor jogging track and completely encloses the inner yard, which is landscaped with shrubs and fruit trees and contains two small houses. Since the floor of the jogging barn is covered with wood chips and the houses are surrounded by the barns, the yard seems to be an area of complete silence.

In 1955 the New York Racing Association assumed ownership of all the buildings at

*Above:* Stables of trainer D. Wayne Lukas

Belmont. The former owners stayed in their old barns, and, if there was a change in personnel, the owners stayed in place and the trainers changed barns. On the other hand, trainer D. Wayne Lukas, known for the elegant maintenance of the barns he uses throughout American racetracks, has a pool of horses owned by several different owners, and, should they change trainers, it is the owners who must seek a different barn. The barns are provided rent-free and are maintained by Belmont so that the NYRA can attract the finest racing stables.

There are forty full-time carpenters who work on the upkeep of the barns and cottages and who provide whatever is needed in terms of repairs and cabinetry for the grandstand.

*Above:* Clubhouse parking area

*Below:* Barn area on Secretariat Avenue

*Overleaf:* The paddock

There is a string of shops built in the 1920s, located on a little hillside opposite a small vegetable garden, that look as if they were built for a film set—an impression that is enhanced by the nearby presence of a flock of ornamental chickens. The shops include a plumbing shop, paint shop, blacksmith's shop (actually a welding shop for track rail), glazier's shop, carpentry shop, and a sign shop. The greenhouses provide summer and fall flowers for the racing seasons—petunias, geraniums, ivy, and poinsettias for Aqueduct's winter racing—and trees for an extensive tree replenishment program. The backstretch staff consists of over 200 people, sixty union tradesmen and a grounds crew of approximately 140 people. There are twenty foremen with crews to take care of the public areas and the barns. Since racing comes first, they tow the starting gates, harrow the track, maintain the grandstand, and garden the public areas. Maintaining and gardening the stable areas comes last. After the Belmont Stakes, the main annual event at Belmont, any plantings that are still in the greenhouses are offered to the barns for their gardens and window boxes or are planted and cultivated by the crew. In addition to the barns and cottages there are about sixty-five other buildings, many of which are small structures of masonry block. According to Olin, these are former blacksmith shops, each with a bellows and two chimneys. "Now all horseshoes are aluminum, and all you have to do is bend them. But earlier every barn had one or two blacksmiths because shoeing the horses was a labor intensive job." These buildings are now small storage houses, and horses are shoed by farriers who travel the streets of the racetrack in small suburban vans.

There is a tunnel from the barn area that leads to the paddock directly behind the clubhouse grandstand. At the back of the paddock is a curved saddling shed, open on both sides so the horses are in view of the public who walk behind the shed, and to the media and owners who are in the restricted area of the paddock. The shape of the walking circle, drawn by architect Arthur Froehlich in his 1963 renovation, is slightly fuller on one end to accommodate an old pine tree supported by guy wires and braces. English ivy grows around the base of the tree, which is encircled with wood and iron benches. At the center of the paddock is a bronze statue of Secretariat, the great 1973 Triple Crown winner, by sculptor John Skeaping. A tiny stadium of tiered stairs overlooks this area, allowing people from the clubhouse to see the walking circle. The area is fenced with ornamental ironwork depicting equestrian scenes.

The yard behind the grandstand is more comfortable than that at any other racetrack. Plenty of trees, television monitors, fine garden furniture, and food are available. It is an area where groups of friends or families with small children come to picnic and relax, and many never go anywhere near the track or the paddock, although both are very conveniently located. There is a large fish pond surrounded by pine and willow trees, left over from an earlier estate. Here people bring deck chairs and spend the afternoon in the sun.

A new grandstand, designed in 1963 by Arthur Froehlich, opened in 1968 after a surprisingly long construction. The cost was $30.7 million for the grandstand and clubhouse, paddock, administration building, and entrance to the Long Island Railroad. The track, barns, and landscaping were inherited from the 1905 racetrack.

*Above*: View from the yard of Rokeby Stable's Round Barn

*Below*: View of the Round Barn yard

*Above*: Masonry barn

Froehlich had designed the Aqueduct Racetrack for the New York Racing Association. It opened in 1959 after three years of construction. Froehlich was also working on a master plan for Saratoga for the NYRA in 1963, and it was assumed that he would be the design architect for Belmont. However, his design work did not please the NYRA board of trustees; Harry F. Guggenheim, who had commissioned the Guggenheim Museum, named for his uncle, Solomon R. Guggenheim, wanted Frank Lloyd Wright's firm, Taliesin, to submit a design. A competition was organized between Froehlich, Taliesin, and the New York firm of Kahn & Jacobs. The fee for Taliesin to develop the design was paid for by Guggenheim privately, according to Mark Costello, a NYRA employee and former draftsman for Kahn & Jacobs. John W. Galbreath, chairman of the building committee, and the trustees viewed the presentations over a three-day period, ultimately choosing Froehlich's design. It addressed, says Costello, the problems inherent in the site of the stand, which required the horses to run into shadows on the homestretch during summer afternoons and which caused the track to thaw late in the spring. Even Froehlich's design had to be modified by shortening the roof. The Taliesin presentation (William Wesley Peters, architect) called for a cable-supported canopy that not only covered the grandstand seats but protected the apron as well. Although the roofing materials specified translucent plastic, even the infield would have been in a shadow; and it is generally thought that this is

*Above*: Wooden barns

why the Taliesin design was eliminated. Taliesin did introduce three innovations for this racetrack. The grandstand was to be built on a suspension system with concrete main frames inclined toward the track. The grandstand was not glassed in, but called for a "wall of air" or "air screen" system with a heated layer of air passed vertically between the seated area and the exterior, plus infrared electric heating so that "all seated persons would enjoy complete all-weather comfort with absolutely no impediment to vision of entire track." Finally, Taliesin proposed that all patrons be stacked up over the finish line. The structural design and materials were contemporary with other such structures in the world; Pier Luigi Nervi in Italy and Felix Candella in Mexico were designing stadiums with suspension systems, and translucent, colored plastic was used by Philip Johnson as roofing for the New York State Pavilion at the 1964 World's Fair. The Taliesin design had six stories, very similar to the new grandstand at Arlington, with a below-ground level for the machinery, an apron level, and four levels for seating, plus a clubhouse promenade at the very top. However, the tiers of seating lined up equally and were shallow. John Manley, of Philip Johnson and Associates, who did the sightline studies for Lincoln Center, says that, at best, only the people in the front row would have been able to see from the Taliesin grandstand. The Kahn & Jacobs model could not be located.

The winning grandstand has four elevations of seating that are graduated and stepped

*Overleaf*: Rokeby Stable's Round Barn

*Above*: Cottage inside the Round Barn

back, with posts that support the roof and divide the upper section. The seating capacity is 30,000. Except for the glassed-in clubhouse restaurant, the grandstand is open and unheated. The back facade, opposite the paddock, is dressed in brick and decorated with arches. Some of these window openings are enclosed in cement and the others are filled with horizontal bands of tinted and clear glass, but the gable end (with ironwork insets), which serves as the clubhouse entrance, demonstrates how beautiful the entire building would be if the arches were open and filled with vertical sections of glass.

42

*Right*: Footpath leading to Horseman's Gate

*Above*: Clubhouse seating area in the grandstand

*Above*: Statue of Secretariat and the saddling shed in the paddock

*Below*: View of the grandstand from the paddock

*Above*: Garden furniture and betting stand behind the grandstand

*Below*: The pond from the original Belmont estate

*Above*: Gravel paths behind the grandstand

# CHURCHILL DOWNS

LOUISVILLE, KENTUCKY

Thoroughbred horses can be traced to three Arabian stallions from Arabia, Persia, and the Barbary States. These horses, named Darley Arabian, Godolphin Arabian, and Bylery Turk, were purchased by Englishmen in about 1700 and bred to some fifty English mares. This was done to produce offspring that combined the speed from the Arabian horses with stamina from the English, thus establishing the breed. The English who settled in the South—in Virginia, South Carolina, Kentucky, and Tennessee—brought with them progeny of these important horses, later establishing Thoroughbred stud farms and building tracks for racing. The Civil War devastated the Southern stud farms, wiping out the bloodlines of many early Thoroughbreds. In Virginia, South Carolina, and Tennessee, racing never fully recovered. Kentucky, on the other hand, was neutral during the Civil War and racing, which had taken place in the state since 1789, continued throughout the war. However, in the early 1870s, the post-Civil War economy was so bad that horse breeders considered closing their farms since they could not get good prices for their Thoroughbred yearlings. Even Woodlawn, an old Louisville track, was forced to close. The establishment of Churchill Downs was a move to revive racing in Kentucky.

Colonel Meriwether Lewis Clark (grandson of William Clark of the Lewis and Clark expedition), a prominent Louisville Thoroughbred breeder, was approached by a group of men with a plan to help stimulate the industry. In 1873 Clark traveled to Europe in search of ideas for the racetrack and keys to the sport's success. Among the famous tracks Clark visited was Epsom Downs in England, where the Epsom Derby is held. Clark decided to model his track after this one and called it Churchill Downs after his great-grandfather, Armstead Churchill, who had owned the land on which the track would be built. Clark decided to organize races by the age and class of Thoroughbreds, another feature of English racing. His stay in Europe extended for a period of two years, and when he returned to America he "knew more about racing than anybody and formulated racing rules for this country," according to Derby historian Jim Bolus. Clark also introduced the French betting system, parimutuels, to this country and was instrumental in getting the necessary legislation passed in 1878 to permit it.

Clark devised the Kentucky Derby as a stakes race for three-year-old horses. It was first

49

run on May 17, 1875, at a distance of a mile and a half. (The length of the race was reduced to 1¼ miles in 1894.) From the very first it was a popular and social occasion, with 10,000 people attending the opening day—a New York paper reported that the grandstand was crowded, the weather good, the women attractive, and the track fast. The first twenty years of Churchill Downs were successful, the only real problems being that the grandstand was badly situated across the track, requiring the racing patrons to face the afternoon sun, and that Clark was financially extravagant (he kept an apartment at the racetrack and entertained in a manner perhaps as excessive as his weight—300 pounds). These problems were remedied when a new grandstand was constructed in 1894–95 and a new manager, Colonel Matt J. Winn, was hired in 1902. Three additional hurdles remained: there was a bookmakers' strike in 1908; James Ben Ali Haggin, a New Yorker with a large racing stable, was personally insulted by a remark made to him during the 1910 Derby and proceeded to mount an Eastern establishment boycott of the race which lasted two decades; and the

*Above*: Post parade for The Breeders' Cup Classic, November 5, 1988

Kentucky Derby was run on the same day as the Preakness (an important race for three-year-old horses held at Pimlico, a racetrack built in 1870 in Baltimore).

Winn, however, was a superb promoter; he travelled to New York and interested racing writers in the Kentucky Derby, and, in 1922, persuaded Benjamin Block, owner of that year's leading horse, to run in the Derby instead of the Preakness. Jim Bolus says that after 1922 the best horses were run in the Kentucky Derby, which eventually superseded the Preakness in importance. It was not until 1930 that the two races were scheduled on separate days, with sufficient time in between so that Gallant Fox, the leading horse, could run in both, and not until 1935 was the idea of the three classic races—the Derby,

*Above*: The grandstand from the backstretch

*Below*: The infield from the grandstand

Preakness, and Belmont—introduced. The name Triple Crown was coined in 1940. By then the Eastern establishment's horses were running at Churchill Downs and the boycott was over. The Kentucky Derby had become the most famous Thoroughbred race in the world. The Kentucky Derby, in fact, has become a racing event so fundamental to American popular culture that the site, Churchill Downs, was designated a National Historic Landmark in 1978.

The 1875 grandstand and clubhouse buildings were designed by Louisville architect John Andrewartha and included two towers to be used as observation posts. The 1894–95 grandstand was constructed on the track's west side, following a design by Joseph D. Baldez, a twenty-four-year-old draftsman in the firm of D.X. Murphy of Louisville. Baldez retained the towers, but elongated them to form octagonal spires. This section is still the central seating area and provides a good view of the track. The rear of the grandstand, facing the paddock, is made of brick and features roundels depicting horse heads in high relief. In

*Above*: The twin spires of The Kentucky Derby Museum

order to ensure absolute success for one afternoon of racing at the most popular race in the world, there are 42,000 seats—12,000 more than at any other racetrack—and a large press box. The grandstand additions date from 1920, 1960, and 1963; in 1967 roof boxes were constructed. In 1924 the clubhouse was extended to its present length. The rear of the grandstand, as seen from the paddock, is dominated by the Italianate detailing of the 1894–95 building and the famous twin spires, but is also laced with stairwells, balconies, and numerous projecting additions.

There were picnics on the infield from the very first Derby Day; tunnels were constructed from the grandstand to the infield in 1937. There has never been any attempt

*Above*: The back of the grandstand from the paddock

*Below*: The saddling shed in the paddock``.

*Overleaf*: The grandstand from the clubhouse turn

*Above*: Saddling shed

to keep the infield clear and uncluttered; it has been filled with tents, tote boards, and flower gardens blocking an otherwise clear view of the race. At one time, a band platform was erected opposite the grandstand and a training track was built inside the main one. The main track is a one-mile oval, the interior turf course is ⅞ mile. In the spring, for Derby Day, tulips abound, some produced by the track's greenhouses and others imported from Holland. Other plantings appear throughout the racetrack, among them petunias, scarlet sage, marigolds, dusty miller, and lantana. There are also numerous flower-filled urns, three of which are from the 1893 World's Columbian Exposition.

In 1961 the Churchill Downs Kentucky Derby Museum was founded, which has a permanent display on the Derby, as well as other racing-related exhibitions. It is currently housed in a building designed in 1985 by E. Verner Johnson of Boston, and incorporates the famous twin spires in its neo-Gothic roof.

*Above*: The homestretch and the finishing post

*Above:* Winner's circle at The Breeders' Cup Turf, November 5, 1988

*Below:* View of the paddock from the saddling shed

*Above*: Grandstand interior, the original Jockey Club

# DEL MAR FAIRGROUNDS AND THOROUGHBRED CLUB

Del Mar Fairgrounds and Thoroughbred Club was built in 1937, commissioned by the state of California for the 22nd District Agricultural Association. Designed by Sam Hamill, the buildings are recreations of the major Spanish Colonial landmarks in the West and Southwest. At the western edge of the Fairgrounds is the East Exhibit Building, a horticultural hall based on San Francisco's Mission Dolores, founded in 1776 by Father Palou. Across the square is the West Exhibit Building, which is a composite of the entrance to the San Gabriel Mission in Los Angeles and a bell tower. There are several other buildings copied from old Spanish ranches in California. At the back of the square is the continuous wall of the cathedral-like grandstand, with walls based on the great buttressed walls of the San Gabriel Mission (although the buttressing has been largely obscured by structural changes). On the eastern end of the grandstand, located on the second town square, is the entrance to the clubhouse. It is a copy of the entrance and tower of the Mission San José de Aguayo, built from 1768 to 1777 near San Antonio, Texas, except that no Rococo saints grace the clubhouse entrance. On the clubhouse square is the Cantina and the most romantic saddling shed found in any of America's racetracks. The saddling shed has a dirt floor, adobe walls, and square posts supporting a roof sheathed in bark-stripped logs, and it is covered in a thickly planted and clipped ivy. The overall plan is like that of a Spanish town with two public squares; the back of the grandstand serves as a backdrop, and the fourth side is open. One of the town squares is surrounded by exhibition halls, for this was foremost a fairgrounds for San Diego County and used for agricultural and horticultural exhibits; the other square is surrounded by racetrack-related buildings.

The racetrack was built at the end of a craze for Spanish Colonial Revival architecture

that Marcus Whiffin, in *American Architecture Since 1780*, traces to San Diego's Panama-California Exposition in 1915 and which reached its apex in 1925. It was built just after the Depression, when state governments were interested in reviving racing as a means of generating income, and at a time when teams of architects and engineers were sent out across the country to measure and record landmarks similar to those recreated here. In terms of labor, Del Mar Fairgrounds and Thoroughbred Club is the largest adobe complex built in modern California's history. An entire hill was excavated to provide materials. The project was a collaboration between the Federal Work Projects Administration (the racetrack and agricultural buildings are constructed of adobe walls) and actors Bing Crosby and Pat O'Brien, who invested $500,000 in the project. Crosby was the president of the racetrack for its first nine years. He cowrote and recorded a theme song for Del Mar called "Where the Turf Meets the Surf." The racetrack is located near a small inlet where the San Dieguito River Basin joins the Pacific Ocean, and above it the streets of the cities of Del Mar and

*Above*: Betting windows

Solano Beach lace the hills, making it possible to look down on the activities at the racetrack.

All these buildings will soon be demolished and completely replaced. The new racetrack is a 1990s recreation of that of the 1930s. The Turf Club entrance will still be based on the Mission of San José de Aguayo, but its tower will be moved up the grandstand and doubled to form a cathedral entrance (like the Zócolo Cathedral in Mexico City) to span the horse walk leading from the paddock to the track. The scale will change dramatically: the royal palms that now overshadow the bell towers of the various buildings will reach the middle of the five-story grandstand. Private sky boxes, an important part of modern sports architecture, will be added. A new lounge will replace the Cantina, and Mission Dolores will give

*Above*: East Exhibit Building

*Below*: Saddling shed

*Above*: Marquee on the highway above Del Mar Fairgrounds

*Below*: West Exhibit Building

way to a building for operations. Adobe will be replaced by plaster over cement, but the roofing will still be Mission tile. On the whole, the plan of the old track and references to the Spanish revival style remain, but Del Mar will now clearly be a racetrack and not an architectural theme park. One building for agriculture and horticultural exhibits replaces four earlier buildings. The architect, Morio Kow (of Froehlich, Kow & Gong, Los Angeles), estimates that it will cost $75 million, which is considerably less than many of the new racetracks. The firm was originally established in 1939 by Arthur Froehlich, who specialized in racetrack architecture. Among his many racetrack projects were Hollywood Park, Aqueduct, and Belmont.

Del Mar Fairgrounds has been expanded at many times, although the move to demolish and rebuild the track has long been considered. Adobe is not a modern material and requires extensive patching, and there are some areas of the grandstand that do not meet the region's seismic codes. The primary reason for the rebuilding is attendance, for both the

*Above*: Pavilion in the parking lot

racetrack and the fairgrounds have grown in proportion to the expansion of San Diego County, one of the largest in the nation. In 1979 Tucker Sadler & Associates, San Diego, was hired to investigate alternatives to demolishing the inadequate grandstand. The grandstand was modified in 1968 and 1974, and enlarged in 1977. The new grandstand will be large, but will be closed on various levels on days when racing is moderate, allowing the operational servicing and staffing costs to be reduced; it will only be fully opened on big racing days. This approach is the opposite of that at the new racetrack at Arlington, which is designed for capacity crowds every day and to be overcrowded on big racing days.

# FAIR GROUNDS RACE COURSE

NEW ORLEANS, LOUISIANA

In archaeological terms, the Fair Grounds Race Course in New Orleans is even older than the track at Saratoga. The site was originally used for the Mechanics and Agricultural Fairs before the Civil War, appearing on contemporary maps as "Fair Grounds." The year after the Civil War it was the location of the Southern States Agricultural and Industrial Exposition, for which its entrance gatehouses were built. The Fair Grounds Race Course was established in 1872 under the auspices of the Louisiana Jockey Club and has been in continuous use since that time. There had been important Thoroughbred tracks in New Orleans in the early nineteenth century, when New Orleans was the fourth-largest city in the nation (Eclipse Course, established in 1837 near what is now Audubon Park, and Metairie Course, now Metairie Cemetery, were the two most important). At least one important Kentucky horse, named Lexington, was shipped there specifically to race, an event that acknowledges the significance of New Orleans in the early history of the sport. The geographical focus of Thoroughbred racing in America has generally been in the Northeast and Kentucky since the Civil War, so that Saratoga in New York (1864), Pimlico in Maryland (1870), and Churchill Downs in Kentucky (from 1875) are considered the more important tracks. But it is precisely the autonomous quality of this track that makes it so interesting.

The Fair Grounds Race Course is located ideally within the city. As the site was used for nineteenth-century agricultural expositions and fairs, the track retains its generic name. Even now, the racetrack hosts the famous New Orleans Jazz Festival, opening its infield to an annual event where numerous concerts take place simultaneously, thereby maintaining its historic function as a fair grounds in this ethnically diverse American city. The track surface also frequently serves as a burial ground for the ashes of track patrons who prefer this site to the aboveground mausoleums throughout the city. The Fair Grounds is composed of a carefully preserved group of buildings, many of which were not designed for the site but have become assimilated into it.

The address of the Fair Grounds is 1751 Gentilly Boulevard. The entrance gate, used by owners, trainers, and horse vans, is flanked by Gothic revival gatehouses designed by New Orleans architect James Gallier, Jr. in 1866 for the Southern States Agricultural and

Industrial Exposition. These buildings, designated as landmarks by the city, are elaborate, oversized, red brick structures with black-and-white painted millwork trim. Between the houses are three masonry posts supporting the iron gates, and the traditional cast-iron jockey with painted silks and outstretched arm marking the entrance. A large yellow, red, and black sign on the fence by this entrance serves as a reminder that the Fair Grounds is the home of Risen Star, the winner of the 1988 Preakness and Belmont Stakes, two of the three most important American races. This great son of New Orleans, sired by Secretariat, brought money and fame to the city when it was disclosed that his earnings, which eventually amounted to three million dollars, were tithed to the Little Sisters of the Poor, one of the city's Catholic charities. Through this gate is a view of the ancient oak trees in the infield and the front of the grandstand. Further down the street is the grandstand entrance gate to the track, which is lined with taxis and sits opposite a neighborhood bar. Gentilly Boulevard is one of the oldest New Orleans thoroughfares, having been laid out along an

*Above*: Gatehouse

Indian path which runs north to Bayou St. John.

Whereas many of the early racetracks seem to have outgrown their environs, this racetrack neither dwarfs nor ignores its neighbors. In particular, Pimlico, Churchill Downs, and Oaklawn are located in residential neighborhoods whose streets, lined with modest, wood-frame houses, can no longer easily handle the heavy traffic on racing days. The Fair Grounds, however, is gently separated by a high, whitewashed, latticed fence built recently by owner Louie Roussel III, who left a few openings in it for neighbors to enter the track directly from their backyard gardens. This fence is one of the best new additions to any of the racetracks in terms of design, property enhancement, security, and generosity of spirit; it

*Above*: The grandstand

*Overleaf*: The turf course and infield

is not uncommon for other tracks to offer only chain link and a cluttered view of the backstretch. Two sides of the Fair Grounds run along old boulevards—Gentilly and Esplanade; each has the capacity to handle four lanes of traffic and is accessible from throughways that traverse the city. A third side of the racetrack is bounded by one of the oldest cemeteries in New Orleans, St. Louis III, which opened in 1854. High tombs and crosses form a baroque backdrop for the horses as they exercise in the barn area. The fourth side is comprised of barns, recently covered with blue-and-white enameled-steel siding.

Esplanade Avenue runs northwest from the French Quarter toward Lake Pontchartrain, passing along the south side of the Fair Grounds. In 1872, the year the racetrack was officially established, a person following Esplanade north from the French Quarter would have travelled a wide, flat road through nearly empty marshland and come upon a farmhouse, now 2306 Esplanade Avenue, whose fields directly survey the racetrack. This farmhouse is where Edgar Degas stayed with his uncle, Michel Musson, when he visited New Orleans for six months in 1873. It is hard to believe that an artist so interested in the French turf did not take note of the activities at the newly formed racetrack, in full view from the farmhouse. The entire area, besides the farmhouse, consisted only of the grandstand, a few buildings, the racetrack, the Luling Mansion, and the St. Louis III Cemetery just beyond. The farmhouse, although it was only rented by the Musson family, is a landmark because of the short residence of Degas. Near the Musson house is another entrance to the racetrack on Mystery Street.

Just beyond Mystery Gate is the Luling Mansion, which was used as the original Jockey Club. It is a tall, Italianate villa, also designed by James Gallier, Jr. This villa was built in 1865 for Florence Luling and was purchased in 1872 by the Louisiana Jockey Club to be used as the clubhouse. The rooftop was an observation deck, and the upper balconies were also used for viewing races, but by today's standards, it is located quite far from the finish line. Evidently its main function was as a men's club. In any case, this mansion is far more elegant than the one or two poshly decorated rooms, called Director's Rooms or Turf Clubs, housed in most modern grandstand structures today. This building remained an isolated villa, with formal gardens stretching to Esplanade Avenue, until about 1912, when small residential structures were built on the surrounding lots, boxing it in. The villa functioned as the Jockey Club until the 1920s, when another structure was built to replace it. Now it is an apartment house, located at 1436 Leda Court, and was designated as a landmark by the Historic Landmarks Commission in 1978. The cast-iron balustrades, meant to look like stone, have been painted silver and replace earlier wooden ones. Only a fragment of the gardens remains. An elaborate oak-leaf-and-acorn ironwork gate has been added on the garden level.

The grandstand was designed in 1905 by local architect Rathbone De Buys for another racetrack in New Orleans, the City Park Race Track, and was moved to its present site in 1919. However, at least five grandstands were erected at the Fair Grounds between its opening in 1872 and the establishment of the present one in 1919. The first was a two-story, wood-frame structure with decorative millwork and was topped by a cupola. A

*Above*: The St. Louis III cemetary from the barn area

*Below*: The grandstand from the infield

second, larger one, equipped with electric lights, was built in 1882. The third was a very grand, iron-and-wood structure that was moved from Union Park in St. Louis following the abolition of horse racing in Missouri in 1907. It measured 365 feet, with several domed towers giving it what has been described as an exotic, Middle Eastern quality. *The Times-Democrat* of December 8, 1907, records that it was "the largest, the most modern, and the most comfortable grandstand at any racetrack south of New York." It was only in use for about five years, however, when it burned in 1918. In 1908 horse racing was prohibited in Louisiana, but it resumed again in 1914. A fourth, temporary grandstand was erected in three days in order to open the 1919 season, and the present stand was reconstructed at the Fair Grounds the same year.

The De Buys grandstand started out as a shingle-style structure with weatherboard siding and decorative gable windows; it now has stucco siding and a tile roof, which was recently replaced with metal sheeting, and no gable windows. In 1926 the Fair Grounds management was taken over by Colonel E.R. Bradley of Kentucky, who added concrete bleachers fronting the grandstand and probably installed the sash windows. This grandstand has the oldest, but possibly the most effective, system of enclosure and ventilation of any American racetrack. The front of the grandstand is enclosed with double-hung, multiple-pane sash windows that work on pulleys and can be stored under the roof. The windows can enclose the grandstand either partially or completely. Windows of the same sort appear to have been used in the 1905 grandstand at Oaklawn in Hot Springs, Arkansas. Since each sash operates independently, one group of patrons can be protected from the weather while another group, a few feet away, can enjoy the fresh air. Completely open, they provide an unobstructed view of the course; completely closed, the space can be air-conditioned. Newer grandstands do not offer these alternatives and do not necessarily afford a better view of the track. In 1953 the De Buys grandstand was extended by flat additions on each end of the roof; the use of the same sash windows made it a very compatible renovation.

The grandstand looks onto an infield that contains some very large, old oak trees with whitewashed trunks, as is the custom in the tropics, or at least in the Victorian tropics. It is an infield so smooth and large that it resembles the pasture lands surrounding the plantations located along the Mississippi River outside New Orleans. Although the trees are large, they do not obstruct the view of the horses. This infield is very much the ghost of the pre-Civil War fair grounds. There is a small, pretty lake, but the traditional landscaping elements common to most racetracks are largely unnecessary and extremely artificial in these surroundings. Clearly, the current owners have looked for decorative fillers. Palm trees have been tried, but since they are not indigenous and are dwarfed by the oaks they provide neither glamour nor authenticity.

Box hedges are used sparingly. On major racing days the horses are saddled in the infield directly across from the paddock in stalls created by tall box hedges. The infield also contains whitewashed obelisks surrounded by trimmed box hedges that mark the graves of two important Louisiana horses, Black Gold and Pan Zareta. Black Gold, winner of the Louisiana, Kentucky, Chicago, and Ohio derbies, was inducted into Saratoga's Racing Hall

*Above*: Obelisks marking the graves of Pan Zareta and Black Gold

*Below*: Lattice fence at the edge of the Fair Grounds

of Fame in 1989. The Fair Grounds program explains that Black Gold was a local favorite, noting that his last race at the Fair Grounds was on January 18, 1929, when he broke his foreleg as he neared the finish line: "With all the stamina that had made him famous, he ran courageously on three legs until his jockey mercifully pulled him up. With his head held high, Black Gold was led to the paddock for the last time." An earlier horse, Pan Zareta, also a member of the Hall of Fame, was a mare that finished first seventy-six times during her career in the early 1900s.

The present clubhouse, built in 1926 under Colonel Bradley's administration, once looked like a Louisiana farmhouse. There was a steeply pitched, red-tile roof decorated with an octagonal cupola. The long facade had a full-length, open veranda or *galerie* along the first story, and a wide outside staircase led to the main rooms on the upper floor. The veranda is now completely glass-enclosed, and the stairs have been removed. The building has been joined to the two large structures on either side, and, in connecting it, a portion of the roof was removed so that the cupola is no longer in the center. The building is further ignobled by being joined to a high-rise, black-tinted, glass-enclosed grandstand built in 1964 called the Turf Club. The Turf Club houses state-of-the-art betting facilities, which means one can watch the races in a quiet, television-monitored interior space that includes a restaurant, a flashy bar, and a betting window that resembles a bank teller's counter. The Fair Grounds Turf Club has a good view of the homestretch and is a carefully designed building. However, no attempt was made to relate this building to the existing grandstand or clubhouse in terms of materials, scale, or design. This is not all that remarkable since it was designed some twenty years before the advent of postmodernism, which demands architectural recognition of a building's place and its past.

The oldest section of the barn area is located near the old Jockey Club and runs north along the cemetery. The earliest barn, a long whitewashed shed, is now the property of Louie Roussel II. The rest of the barns spread north along the cemetery and east along the far side of the track and form a fairly dense grid of passageways from the barns to the track entrance. There is a rubber bridle path down the center of these asphalt streets; horses have the right of way before any vehicle. It is an exotic piece of urban landscape. Loudspeakers carry daily Mass to the stable hands and hot walkers; a resident priest, who wears blue jeans and a belt buckle that says "God," attends to the spiritual needs of those who live on the backside of the track and counsels against drug abuse. Mass is also held on Sundays in the ground-floor restaurant of the clubhouse, and is attended by the frontside staff, waiters and waitresses, grounds crew, valets, and various executives. Betting-window clerks, parking attendants, and jockeys seem to breeze in a few hours later, closer to post time.

*Above*: The Luling Mansion

# GULFSTREAM PARK

The racetrack at Hallandale had a rocky start. When it opened for racing on December 1, 1944, it already had a five-year history of financial problems. The track was planned and organized by Joseph Smoot, with no known backers, and built by John C. Horning, a local contractor who built many homes in Hallandale. When the track closed almost immediately (it opened on February 1, 1939, and closed four days later because the public preferred Hialeah, which had better horses), Horning assumed ownership (sixty-two percent), which represented his $1.5 million investment. On February 7, Horning sought capital, but could not issue stock because the Florida Securities Commission determined that it was an unsound venture. He declared bankruptcy on February 11. In May 1944, James Donn, a Miami florist, bought Gulfstream for $100,000, assuming $750,000 in liabilities, and was joined by George Langford and other stockholders who added another one million dollars.

During the first ten years of the racetrack Donn devoted a great deal of effort to landscaping. "It is in the landscaping and beautification of the track that the real changes have been made. During our first year there wasn't a tree or shrub to relieve the barren waste. Today more than 800 royal palms have been planted, tropical plants, and shrubbery," Donn said in a 1955 interview in *Turf & Sports Digest*. His floral business, Exotic Gardens, had a landscape division which had supplied the plantings for south Florida estates in the 1910s and 1920s, and the landscaping at Gulfstream became the highlight of the track. By the 1950s the fine collection of royal palms had been established (the trees were imported from Davie, Florida, where they had been planted in the 1920s and 1930s). The track now has 350 of these trees, significant in view of the fact that Miami lost many of its palms to disease in the 1970s. Gulfstream treated all their palms, accounting for their survival. There are also coconut palms and hundreds of varieties of plants. Small, circular flower beds with annual plantings dotted the infield in the 1950s and have now been moved to the paddock area. The infield lake has a miniature Mississippi riverboat, the Suwannee Queen, and brightly colored sailboats.

A new clubhouse and grandstand were built in 1955 (Robert M. Little, Miami, architect) and the facilities were enlarged and improved through the 1980s by the veteran Miami architectural firm of Steward & Skinner. The 1955 grandstand had a cantilevered

*Above*: Post parade at The Breeders' Cup, November 4, 1989

roof and a seating capacity of 7,500. Little also designed a clubhouse, which is incorporated in the present buildings and retains its distinctive 1950s entrance. During the 1960s the back of the grandstand was gradually modified from a glass wall to a largely enclosed facade to which a long balcony was added in the 1980s. The paddock was relandscaped, jockeys' quarters were built, and a pavilion restaurant was added on the clubhouse turn. The restaurant has several terraces on the ground level, which are covered with a tensile roofing made of a Teflon-covered polyester fabric. The upper terraces have a number of individual tents covered in Teflon-coated, striped canvas.

*Right*: South Pavilion

*Above and below*: The paddock at The Breeders' Cup, November 4, 1989

*Right*: The paddock   *Overleaf*: The barns

*Above*: View from the grandstand

*Below*: The grandstand and apron seating

*Above*: The Breeders' Cup Classic, November 4, 1989

# HIALEAH PARK

Hialeah, one of the most beautiful sports facilities in the United States, is the product of an ideal marriage between client and architect. Joseph Widener, a Philadelphia philanthropist, art collector, and benefactor of the National Gallery of Art, purchased a small racetrack in the city of Hialeah, northwest of Miami Beach, in 1931.

Hialeah was not a particularly convenient location for bettors or horsemen; located forty miles south of West Palm Beach, it was far away from the wealthy and glamorous patrons Widener wished to attract. He guessed, however, that his own drawing power would bring them to Hialeah anyway, and his hunch was largely correct. To facilitate the process, he decided to create an exquisite backdrop for those who shared his interest in racing.

Through his agent, Major Warburton, Widener hired a young architect, Lester Geisler, to design an entirely new facility. Geisler, a New Yorker, was the protégé of society architect Addison Mizner (1872–1933) and had joined the Palm Beach firm in 1924. Trained as an engineer, Geisler was only twenty-eight when Mizner made him the design architect of the Cloister Inn in Georgia. Although the firm was renowned for its Spanish Colonial Revival buildings, Geisler says that Mizner told him in 1928 that "everybody can build Spanish, from now on we must do French."

Widener's program was to start fresh, giving the new racetrack a fine Spanish touch. "The first day I met Widener, he wanted some elegant stairways going down from the grandstands to the paddock," notes Geisler. "I made sketches. He was delighted and showed them to his friends." Once Geisler was confident that Widener liked his work, he was able to introduce the idea of building in a French style, using as prototypes buildings illustrated in a 1924 book, *French Provincial Architecture, As Shown in Various Examples of Town & Country Houses, Shops & Public Places Adaptable to American Conditions*, by Philip Lippincott Goodwin and Henry Oothovt Milliken. Geisler selected a small plate depicting outbuildings at the Loire château, Azay-le-Rideau, as representative of his overall vision for the new racetrack. He added that "French is a background for beautiful women and Thoroughbred horses." Widener conceded that he liked French architecture and agreed that Geisler should build Hialeah in a French style, telling him that he must design it to the very best of his ability.

The new racetrack had to be constructed in roughly six months, between June 4, 1931, the closing day of the existing racing season, and January 17, 1932, the opening day of the next season. However, no work could be done until the parimutuel bill was passed in the

*Left*: Stairs from the paddock to the grandstand

state legislature. Geisler, having never been to France before, was given $2,000 by Widener to go to France to study architecture and landscaping. Although maintaining that "I got my feeling for French architecture by traveling through this book," Geisler learned the specifics of French design on this trip. He made numerous sketches, recording details, proportions, colors, and materials, and went to see the racetracks in and around Paris, among them the beautiful course at Longchamps.

In 1929 and 1930, the crash of the stock market wiped out most potential clients for architects. The streets were full of good architects, either unemployed or working as draftsmen. Geisler, then thirty-one, notes that most of the people he hired to work on Hialeah were older and more experienced than he. Widener wanted to employ as many people as possible; as his chief draftsman, Geisler hired New York architect Augustus Betschick and an additional sixteen architects from the Palm Beach area to help develop his plans. Geisler took a flat fee of $6,000, "not much of a design fee but wonderful money in 1931." The others were paid thirty dollars a week, with Betschick earning fifty dollars a week. Major Warburton, the first president of the track, was instrumental in contracting the various construction, landscaping, and engineering firms in order to build this entire racing environment in six months.

To study the elements of racetrack design, and especially the course itself, Geisler went to the old tracks at Belmont and Saratoga Springs. However, there was nothing written on how to build a $1\frac{1}{8}$-mile track. No one knew for sure how far a horse ran from the inside of the rail, and there was no rule to determine the correct distance at that time. Geisler watched and calculated, finally deciding that five feet off the rail would be his measurement for a $1\frac{1}{8}$-mile track. The result is that any horse running three feet off the inside rail, which is the normal distance, is automatically on a fast track. This largely unknown piece of information no doubt contributes to Hialeah's reputation as a fast track. Geisler contracted the same firm that had built the earlier track and knew the drainage and particularities of the site. He gave his specifications to the engineers for the $1\frac{1}{8}$-mile course. The texture of the track, which gives the horse the pressure to push ahead, is a very successful combination of native topsoil from a formula developed by the engineers and grounds crew. The same formula is maintained today.

Much of the genius of Hialeah is in the landscaping. Widener expressed strong opinions regarding the paddock, the infield, and the approach avenues—the three most important elements of racetrack landscape design. Geisler drew the plans, but the final execution was carried out by landscape architect H. L. Clark. Clark knew the location of the most beautiful and durable materials in Florida. He carefully researched the source for the cyprus wood used for the latticed back of the grandstand. Made from the center hardwood of carefully selected trees, the latticework shows none of the usual decay of a tropical climate over time. The royal palms that line the avenues leading to the clubhouse and grandstand entrances were brought by truck from the west coast of Florida, and Australian pines delineate all the boundaries throughout the track.

The barns, in the shape and quantity of their stalls, were modeled after those at

*Above*: The clubhouse entrance terrace   *Overleaf*: Back of the grandstand

Belmont, but the roofs are French. They have a low pitch at the sides, but a high pitch at the ends. Geisler says that Clark had a sense of balance, never allowing "barns too close or too far away from his trees. He would make allowances for spacing trees in relation to the buildings." Widener requested long avenues throughout his racetrack. Nowhere is this more successful than the bridle path, lined with soft-needled Australian pines that lead from the barns to the paddock.

The paddock is now heavily paved with walkways, terraces, and two fountains, and contains a walking ring surrounded by metal railings and cement viewing tiers. Originally, it was designed as an open stretch of grass. According to Geisler, "Mr. Widener's view was a succession of uncluttered areas. He liked it open. Then he liked a very careful placing of very pretty palm trees. It was not just bare open, but it was substantially open. You got the feeling of expansion."

The paddock has many functions; there, the horses are saddled, the owner has his last

*Above*: Clubhouse entrance drive

moment with the jockey and trainer, and the patrons are able to see the horses for the first and only time of the day before making a swift appraisal of their condition and temperament in order to place a bet. At Hialeah this can be accomplished easily by descending the wide stairways that lead from the back of the grandstands to the paddock, and crossing the grass to view the horses as they are saddled or as they circle before entering the tunnel to the track. The horses can also be seen through the latticed arches, covered with bougainvillea, that directly overlook the paddock. Although greatly increased in proportion, these arches are a reincarnation of those at Azay-le-Rideau, which are covered in wisteria and illustrated in *French Provincial Architecture*. The horses are easily visible to clubhouse and general

*Above*: Grandstand entrance drive

*Below*: Grandstand from the backstretch

*Above*: Clubhouse terrace

*Above*: Balcony overlooking the paddock

grandstand patrons alike.

Likewise, Widener viewed the infield as an area between oneself and the horses. His idea was to have a clear and unobstructed view of the track and the running of the horses. When Geisler was asked how he came up with his design, he said, "God and I got together and designed the infield." But it was Widener who allowed him a small lake and no other distractions, except a very few palm trees. The flamingos in the infield were also Widener's idea. Imported from Cuba in 1931, many of the flamingos flew away or died in the early years, but after four or five years they established themselves and began breeding. The early flamingos were considered pretty and incidental and not the symbol of the track that they have become today.

"The grass area that I left open was used as a turf track," says Geisler, who remembers that Widener was not especially interested in grass or turf running, which was only really introduced in the early 1940s, although there had been a turf course at the earlier track.

*Above*: Terrace at the clubhouse entrance

Flower beds were used to break the monotony of the expanse of grass and to designate the homestretch. All the additions in the present park, which consist of three extra islands, numerous palm trees, elliptical box hedges, and a large tote board, are variations on the original, cleanly landscaped infield and dirt track surrounded by high Australian pines.

The gem of the racetrack was the tiny, posh, and beautiful clubhouse, now demolished. Geisler immediately received an A.I.A. design award for this little French palace. The entrance was inspired by the Annex to the City Hall, Ivry-sur-Seine, Paris. The clubhouse was a single-story building, with a recessed entrance flanked by quoin pilasters. The tall entrance doors, topped by an elliptical arch, were copied by Betschick from a bookplate and

*Above*: The clubhouse

*Below*: Administration offices and jockey building

*Overleaf*: Back of the clubhouse

were carved in mahogany. The clubhouse was built, however, to hold 300 people and was admittedly exclusive. It served well for ten years, but the period of great expansion at Hialeah in the late 1940s soon rendered the clubhouse too small. It was demolished in 1948 in order to make way for a larger one.

Also built in 1931 were the jockeys' building and saddling shed. The jockeys' building defines one edge of the paddock, and has a central clock and steeple, and French doors that originally led onto the path to the saddling shed. (Recent renovations have changed all the facade openings.) A long row of stalls facing onto the paddock constitutes the saddling shed. It has painted plaster walls, with circular windows at intervals high on the wall. The horses enter the paddock in the center of this shed row through a high gate that leads directly to the barn area. The paddock at Hialeah is conveniently located to the barns and is probably the best located paddock of any American racetrack. The gateposts and shed roof are covered with bougainvillea. Again, the overall effect recalls the hunting lodge at Azay-le-Rideau.

Pre-cast stone is used to form the balustrades, the quoins, the wide steps, and all the other decorative stone detailing throughout the racetrack. The surface of this stone, called keystone, is made of cement and pulverized natural stone from the Florida Keys. It has a good color and the illusion of being richly veined. The walls are painted plaster. The original roofing material for the clubhouse was dark, fired slate. Geisler claims to have rejected Florida tiles for being "too sameish in color. They looked too new and out-of-place." He was contacted by a prominent Georgia tile maker who had stacks of discarded, mismatched roofing tiles which he sent to Hialeah. Geisler says, "We laid out a few on the ground. They were beautiful in their delicate color variations. They made the loveliest tile roofs you ever saw!"

The cost of the 1931 project was $1.2 million. Geisler recalls that there were virtually no cost overruns and that the people he was dealing with had enough vision to understand the scope of the project. Betschick was familiar with French architecture from previous work in New York, the Island Landscape Company was ably managed by Tinsley Halter, all the parimutuel or mechanized betting machinery was designed and developed by an Australian firm which supplied the equipment and provided the design specifications for the betting windows; the track was built by the same engineering firm that had constructed the earlier track, and the stone casting was handled by a local firm. There was very little steelwork because Geisler was able to use an extended version of the existing grandstand. The project was finished on time; most of the construction of the new track occurred between June 1931, when betting was legalized in the state of Florida, and January 17, 1932. During an economic depression, great quantities of money can be made at a racetrack, so the horses ran on opening day, as promised.

Major building changes took place at the racetrack between 1948 and 1954. Each year a construction project was added in the off-season, greatly expanding the facilities of the track. The most spectacular changes were made in the grandstand itself. After the demolition of the little clubhouse, an entire wing was added to the south end of the grandstand; on its

*Above and below*: The barn area

*Overleaf*: Bridle path

north end the grandstand was increased by nineteen trusses and enclosed in the rear to look like a large château. The earlier grandstand was reroofed, and two important fountains were built. Again, *French Provincial Architecture* was brought into use. The new clubhouse entrance has horseshoe-shaped steps which lead to the second story and out into the boxes. The clubhouse is based on the little Château Vitry in Paris, a small building with a flat, balustraded roof. The ground-floor entrance hall and stairwell is based on the Annex to the City Hall, Ivry-Sur-Seine, Paris. At the end of the long avenue of royal palms (a distance of about three city blocks), are the gatehouses, which mark the entrance to the drive up to the clubhouse steps.

To the back of the clubhouse, which overlooks the paddock, Geisler added an elliptical bay, to give "variety in facade and a tendency, with an outward curve, to see more, psychologically, than with a straight line, from inside." This long, curved, and arched bay creates a shallow, open dining terrace on the upper story and is enclosed by a railing bearing

*Above*: Weighing station

Widener's initials (JW) on the second story, forming an intimate balcony.

The final large building project was added to the northernmost section of Hialeah—the back of the general grandstand. Four stories of betting halls and restaurants project out into the lawn near the grandstand entrance. The circular windows, steep, dormered roofs, and wide quoins all recall Azay-le-Rideau, the royal hunting lodge that was the consistent inspiration for Hialeah for over twenty-five years.

Landscape architecture has a semi-successful history at Hialeah Park. The Widener Fountain is located directly in front of the curving stairwell at the clubhouse entrance. Erected in the 1940s, the fountain is made of cast stone and is sided by bronze plaques

*Above:* Exercise yard

*Below:* Entry gate to the paddock

representing Widener's diverse interests: sports, philanthropy, arts, and architecture. However, another fountain marks the decline in the design code that had held firm at Hialeah. Geisler was working for another owner, Eugene Mori, a financier who bought the track in 1954, and was commissioned to design a simple, low basin that he describes as being in the wrong scale, the wrong style, and the wrong site. "The fountain ought to be somewhere else. It is located where people come into the grandstand from the parking lot. When the fountain was running and the wind was blowing, everybody got wet, so then they had to stop the water so people could get in without getting soaked," Geisler recalls. This fountain, without water, was an unimpressive hole in the ground. In the 1960s, after Geisler was no longer the architect and technical advisor of the track, a Spanish Baroque, three-tiered pedestal, made of cast stone and decorated with life-size bronze flamingos, was placed in the basin and christened the Flamingo Fountain. Though the water is rarely turned on people enjoy the fountain as a place to meet, even though it consumes Widener's "open

*Above*: The Widener Fountain

stretch of grass" and dwarfs the surrounding architecture.

The most obvious modification of the early buildings is the enclosing of the open terraces along the clubhouse roof. Once, big gables hovered over the flat roof of the clubhouse, giving it the exciting illusion of being an industrial shed abutting a small palace. It was an immensely urban look, suggesting the dense commingling of the architecture of several centuries. Now, sliding-glass windows enclose the dining terrace overlooking the paddock and seal the two parts together, but detract from the older building. Some of the circular windows have been replaced with pictorial stained glass, which is sometimes attractive but hardly necessary. A little more successful are the etched-glass walls that form

*Above*: Terrazzo floor in the grandstand

*Below*: Betting windows in the clubhouse

*Overleaf*: Latticed arches overlooking the paddock

*Above and below*: The Turf Club

*Above*: The Flamingo Fountain

*Below*: Clubhouse from the Flamingo Island in the infield

# W. C. STEPHENS

| NAME | RIDER | SET | WORKOUTS |
|---|---|---|---|
| Tough Bird | Nelson | 4 | G ? |
| Don Hernando | Sal | 3 | G |
| Free Getaway | Wacker | 2 | G |
| Cefis | Wacker | 3 | B |
| Posen | | 4 | W |
| Silvery Topping | Ella | 1 | WGG |
| Creme Fraiche | Nelson | 2 | GG |
| Conquilot | Nelson | 1 | G |
| Figure | Sal | 4 | B |
| Samerkand | Wacker | 4 | GG |
| Devilish Grin | Wacker | 4 | G |
| | | | |
| Gild | — | 1 | W |
| Tagish | Ella | 2 | WGG |
| Nicholas | Sal | 1 | GG |
| ReDe Slew | — | 4 | |
| Kokand | | 2 | W ✓ |
| Mia Duchessa | — | 2 | W ✓ |
| Duck Creek | — | 1 | W ship |
| Demonry | Nelson | 3 | G |
| Roi Danzig | — | — | W |

*Above*: Terrace overlooking the gap

the Turf Club on the clubhouse roof, located directly opposite the flamingo island in the infield.

The modern Hialeah Park had promoted the flamingo as its theme. Somehow, this is not surprising. It merely reflects the evolution of the racecourse from its traditional role as a place to watch races to one of a theme park, where the modern-day patron seems more at home watching the race on a television in the clubhouse restaurant than standing at the trackside or sitting in the grandstands.

*Left*: Workout schedule at Woody Stephens' barn

*Above:* Jockeys' quarters

*Below:* Men's room in the clubhouse

*Above*: The Barber Shop

*Above*: Patrons

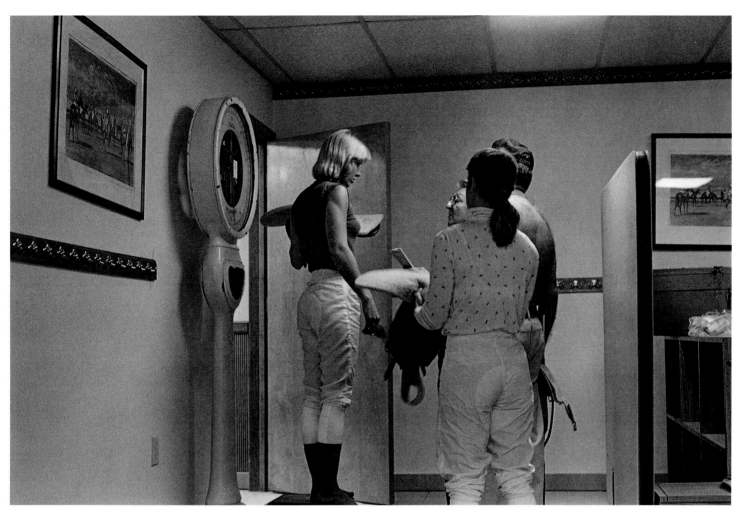

*Above and below*: Women jockeys

*Overleaf*: Jockeys' quarters

# KEENELAND RACE COURSE

LEXINGTON, KENTUCKY

Keeneland is perhaps the most international of the American racetracks; its four annual Thoroughbred auctions are attended by owners and breeders from Japan, Australia, the Middle East, and Europe. It is small, retaining aspects of a country house, socially exacting, and, to a degree, independently wealthy. It is located in an area renowned for breeding classic horses, and runs two racing meetings totalling a thirty-one-day period each year.

Although the present track was organized in 1936, it is actually a continuation of a private racetrack built by John Oliver (Jack) Keene in 1916. The gateposts come from the Kentucky Association track, constructed in Lexington in 1826, which replaced racetracks dating from 1787. At Keeneland's core are three connected buildings constructed of limestone, with flat roofs and ironwork ornamentation. Expansions in 1936, 1953, 1963, 1984, 1986, and 1990 are references to that early, straightforward architecture. The site, the dimensions of the main track, and the paddock's walking ring are remnants of Keene's private racetrack complex. The placement of the structures has not been altered. The clubhouse is at the head of the homestretch rather than at the first turn, as it is in all other American racetracks, and the grandstand faces west instead of east. Both these deviations seem sensible, since a good view of the horses as they move toward the finish is, after all, the heart of the matter, and facing the sun during the late afternoon on a chilly April or October day, when Keeneland runs its meetings, is more of a pleasure than a hardship.

Keene knew the world of racing and was the designer of the original racetrack. Raised in Lexington, Keene had become internationally known after training horses in Russia in the stables of Henri Block and Michael Lazeroff in 1902–03. Lazeroff's horse, Irish Lad, had won an important series of races in Warsaw, Moscow, and St. Petersburg (now Leningrad). He also trained and raced horses in California and Japan, where he won seventeen races with American Thoroughbreds. He returned to Lexington in 1909 and trained horses at the Kentucky Association track, located on Fifth Street. During that time he planned his "dream" track, which he began to construct in 1916. He was neither a rich man nor a man who wanted to develop his private track commercially, but, as W.T. Bishop, Keeneland's first track manager, said, he was "a man who wished to have a private racetrack where he could invite his friends, where they could bring their horses and race against each other even. If

129

*Above*: The grandstand from the infield

racing were outlawed on all the racetracks in the nation or if racing was declared to be illegal or illicit or otherwise, his thing was that he would have some kind of place where he could continue to operate and that he could continue to own horses, breed horses, produce horses, race horses, train horses—do all those kinds of things."

By 1933, when the Kentucky Association track closed after falling into general disrepair, Keene's racetrack was still unfinished after nearly twenty years and $400,000 worth of construction. Keene had run out of money and Lexington did not have a racetrack. Although Thoroughbred racing was experiencing an economic boom elsewhere, neither Keene nor the people of Lexington wanted an extremely commercial track, nor was it particularly easy to raise money for another track in the middle of the Depression. A deal was struck, however, and Lexington got the racetrack it desired. Historian James Charleton describes the founding of Keeneland this way: "Many of Lexington's city fathers favored reviving racing in the city. They felt the extinction of racing in the heart of Thoroughbred racing country was unconscionable. Major Louie A. Beard, Jack Young, Hal Price Headley, and James Bassett, Jr., were leading figures. They envisioned a new kind of track, to be operated by a nonprofit association, with racing conducted for the benefit of those most concerned—the horsemen—and with the profits to be turned back into the track and good works for the community. Keene's private racing complex was chosen as the site of the new

*Above:* Grandstand and paddock (center), main track and infield (middle), sales pavilion (lower right), and barns and training track (top)

venture. Recognizing, in the character of the new venture, a 'kinship of ideas,' Keene sold the property to the newly formed Keeneland Association at a bargain price."

The corporation, formed in April 1935, purchased the property in August of that year. In June the drive to raise $350,000 for the racetrack began by offering preferred-capital stock for $100 per share. By October 15, 1936, $305,000 was collected from the sales of preferred stock and an additional $55,000 from the sales of memberships.

In October 1935, after reviewing submissions by three local architects, the corporation hired Robert W. McMeekin to develop his design for an adaptation of the clubhouse, new jockeys' quarters, and a new grandstand. Keene's original buildings comprised three adjacent structures with living quarters, a clubroom, and stalls on the ground level. At the center was the clubroom, a square structure of two stories with a flat roof, which McMeekin modified by adding a slate, gabled roof and a portico at the clubhouse entrance. Connected to the structure are two three-story wings, which are linked by stone arcades containing horse stalls. McMeekin added a deep wooden porch of two levels to the western wing overlooking the track, creating a small grandstand. His clubhouse entrance is a hall containing a stairwell leading to a restaurant and the grandstand boxes. It is the finest clubhouse entrance of any American racetrack. It is supremely comfortable, having once been part of a country house, and not too stylish—the overhead chandelier, for instance, is a

131

*Overleaf:* The grandstand

converted wagon wheel. Warm, honey-colored afternoon light pours through the windows of the clubhouse, making it a comfortable place to meet friends and watch people arrive. McMeekin designed a grandstand of limestone and wood which seats 2,500 people, and the gable end is comprised of a series of arches repeated throughout the racetrack buildings. McMeekin was the architect for the expansion of the grandstand in 1953, which was extended to the north after the old field stand was demolished.

In May 1936, as part of the capital drive, memberships were offered to the Keeneland Club by invitation only; a lifetime membership was $500 and an associate membership was fifty dollars a year. Life membership required no further dues, entitled the member access to the clubhouse and any part of the grounds, and two seats on the "Club Balcony." Membership passes to a surviving spouse upon death of a member, and can be willed to one child upon the death of both mother and father. If the member dies without a will, life membership in the Keeneland Club passes to the oldest child, or ceases when there are no children. Associate memberships allowed admittance to the clubhouse, were annual, and non-transferable. A list of members printed in the *Lexington Herald* on October 15, 1936, consisted of life members primarily from Lexington and New York, as well as owners of other racetracks throughout the country, such as Dr. Strub, Hal Roach, and Joseph Widener, and associate members almost entirely consisted of people from Lexington and Cincinnati, Ohio.

James E. Bassett III, Chairman of the Keeneland Association, thinks that much of the money was really collected "in kind," in the form of building materials, labor, and equipment from the community. He suggests that cash raised from the sale of shares went toward the purchase of the land and buildings from Keene, and that it was only at the very end of the project that additional money was raised by selling life memberships. Bassett insists that the development of the racetrack was a community effort and that the "spirit of Keeneland" was formed during those days, "contributing to the betterment of the industry, and the desire to build a jewel that would reflect on the community." In the spirit of a nonprofit organization, no officer or director received compensation during their first thirty years of service. Also, the racetrack acts as a landmark in the area. Company and family picnics are traditionally held on the grounds, and during the fall meet, by a mutual arrangement, Saturday football games are played at night at the nearby University of Kentucky so as not to interfere with attendance at the track. The gambling statistics per capita at Keeneland are the lowest in the Thoroughbred industry. Keeneland is primarily a social place. Most of its capital improvements are to expand facilities for the largely private use of owners and breeders from the surrounding farms, and for corporate use. Also, Keeneland invests in its stakes races in order to attract good racing.

Unlike that of Hialeah or Santa Anita, the style of Keeneland is conveyed, not through its architecture, but through its resolution to remain anchored in the Kentucky landscape and its focus on the sport. Keeneland is so famous for its adherence to tradition that even simple features—some inherited, others expensively conceived—take on a certain grandeur.

The main track, as laid out by Keene, is 1 1/16 miles in circumference, which makes the far

*Above*: Gatepost from the Kentucky Association

*Below*: Ironwork balcony on the clubhouse

side of the track much more visible than one measuring 1½ miles, such as the course at Belmont Park. In 1936 an infield lake was created, but was drained the following year because of an untoward glare produced by the afternoon sun on the water surface. The present infield landscaping, which includes a generous grouping of flowering fruit trees, is in the lake bed and therefore below the sight line of track. A patron standing at the rail can watch the entire race without obstruction.

The turf course, built in 1984, follows the natural contours of the land, resulting in an innovative course that drops thirteen feet on the backside along the lake edge and resumes until it gradually drops twenty inches between the final turn and the finish line, creating a downhill thrust to the finish. This sort of course, although confined in an American oval, is closer to European courses which follow the terrain. The turf track includes a top layer of fourteen inches of sand for drainage (a composition similar to the track at the Fair Grounds, which withstands the torrential rains from the Gulf of Mexico) to accommodate the spring

*Above*: The Keeneland Club, called the "Clubhouse Entrance"

rains of Kentucky. This depth of sand plus a system of pipes effectively drains in one hour what would normally require six.

Keeneland has cultivated the sense of uninterrupted bluegrass pastures uniting the racetrack to the surrounding farms. This is accomplished by keeping a black barn, indigenous to Kentucky tobacco farms, as a focal point when viewed from the stands and by adding over 1,000 acres to the original 147 to protect that view. When new barns were built in 1981–82 in the area of the main track, they were sunken in order to remove them from sight and retain the view beyond. These barns have convenient access to the main track and are linked directly to the training track, built in 1954.

*Above*: The Keeneland Club, called the "Clubhouse Entrance"

*Below*: The library in the administration building

When Queen Elizabeth II visited in 1984, Keeneland built a half-oval winner's circle so that she could present the trophy in comfort. It is a small area carved out of the apron floor of the grandstand. Set in rusticated field stone floored in sawdust, it is enclosed by a low iron fence. This replaced a circle drawn in the dirt by the chalkman, who, with a muslin bag of chalk and flour on a string with a peg, created the winner's circle after each race. Most of the other tracks had devised more sophisticated circles years earlier, but Keeneland considered it unnecessary until the royal visit, when they needed to provide security and protect the Queen's shoes if it rained. Keeneland normally holds the presentation awards for stakes races in the infield so that everybody in the stands can easily see the horse, jockey, trainer, owners, and the silver cup, plate, or bowl that is placed on a little table covered in black-and-orange felt cloth. The grounds crew place a series of skiffs across the dirt track, providing a bridge to the grass on the other side.

The reason for the Queen's trip to America was to visit her broodmares at Lane's End

*Above*: The backstretch from the grandstand

Farm. She had been advised to breed her mares with American stallions to increase the speed of the progeny. Therein lies the importance of this small area of Kentucky to the worldwide Thoroughbred industry: it is the home of the fastest and strongest pedigreed horses in the world, with a concentration of premier stallions and 8,000 broodmares living on surrounding farms.

The consignment of horses for auction, primarily from the nearby farms, is the major business conducted at Keeneland and is commonly referred to as "the Sales." During the Second World War, when it became impossible to ship horses to Saratoga for the annual

*Above*: The training track

*Below*: The paddock's saddling shed

*Above*: Skiffs leading to the infield

August sales, horses were sold at Keeneland by the Breeders' Sales Company, which was absorbed by the Keeneland Association in 1962.

After 1963 Keeneland become a much larger and more visually sophisticated complex. Racetrack architect Arthur Froehlich of Beverly Hills was hired to make a master plan for its expansion. In that year the grandstand was greatly increased, making it a continuous unit filling the large area from the clubhouse to the grandstand. The materials were glass and steel, and the repeating arches, retained from the original grandstand, were reintroduced by Froehlich on the clubhouse addition facing the paddock. He also designed a single-story office wing which tied into the Keene building and enclosed the east side of the paddock; it was increased to two stories in 1984. Also in 1984 he filled in the space along the southern edge of the walking ring to create a restaurant. The units have flat roofs and are dressed in rusticated limestone, while a continuous series of arches repeats McMeekin's treatment of the gable end of the grandstand. The overall effect is that of entering a seminary or a quadrangle on a small college campus.

Appropriately, there is a library at Keeneland. It was started in 1939 with the gift of 2,300 volumes from William Arnold Hanger, a trustee and director of Keeneland. The current collection has 6,000 volumes and is composed of stud books, racing periodicals, and a major archive of the work of photographer Charles Cook.

*Above*: Award presentation in the infield

In 1984, as part of a building program planned for the fiftieth anniversary of the track (which was hastened a bit by the Queen's visit), a tower and projecting addition, which directly overlook the saddling area, were added, and a glass-enclosed restaurant called the Kentucky Room was added to the roof of the grandstand. Throughout, a solar, bronze-tinted glass is used to reduce glare. The tinted glass takes on a black quality in the sunlight, blending with the Kentucky landscape of creosoted barns and fences. In 1990 a fourth floor was added to the roof area, overlooking the paddock and reflecting the addition of 1984. There are three dining rooms on one side and twenty-two corporate boxes facing the race-track.

In 1970 Arthur Froehlich was asked to design a sales pavilion. It is a circular building of limestone and timber located just below the racetrack on the slight crest of a hill, directly in front of and above the barn area. The building recalls an arena: at the center is a dais holding the auctioneer's stand, and the sales ring is enclosed by ropes. The horses enter on a ramp from the holding area, are led in front of the auctioneer's stand where they are sold, and exit on a ramp directly to the barns. Radiating off the central theater are telephone rooms, conference rooms, bars, cashiers, a pedigree information booth, and cloakrooms. The walls are hung with paintings of horses. The Selected Yearling Sale, held in July, offers horses less than a year old chosen on the basis of pedigree and conformation (their physical charac-

141

teristics). It generally commands the highest prices of any Thoroughbred auction in the world. The November sales are of breeding stock and include individual stakes winners, dispersals of estates, and stallion shares. Over the years, major dispersals have included the horses of H.H. The Aga Khan, Spendthrift Farm, C.V. Whitney, Hermitage Farm, Nelson Bunker Hunt, and Eugene Klein. Keeneland's wealth is derived from these sales—during the racetrack's extensive building expansion in the 1980s, no loans were needed to finance the capital improvements.

*Above*: The winner's circle

*Above*: The paddock

*Below*: The grandstand entrance gate

*Above:* Patrons

*Right*: View of the paddock from the grandstand terraces  *Overleaf*: The paddock

*Above*: The jockeys' quarters

*Below*: The steam room

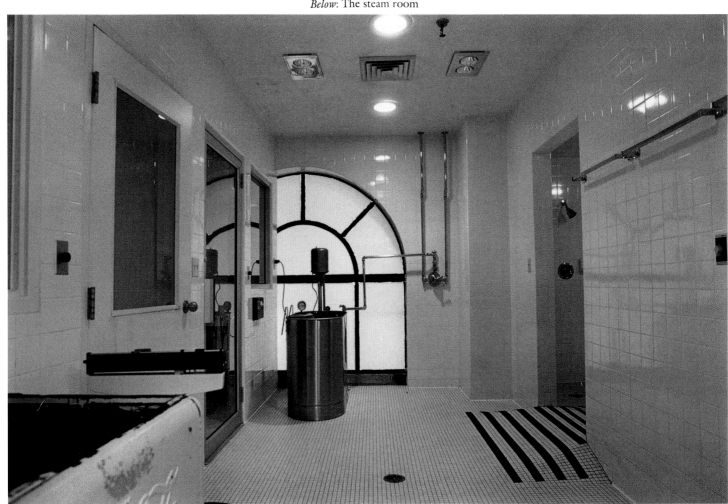

*Above*: The barns

*Above*: Paul Mellon with trainer Mackenzie Miller and jockey Pat Day

*Below*: Keeneland Chairman James E. Bassett III

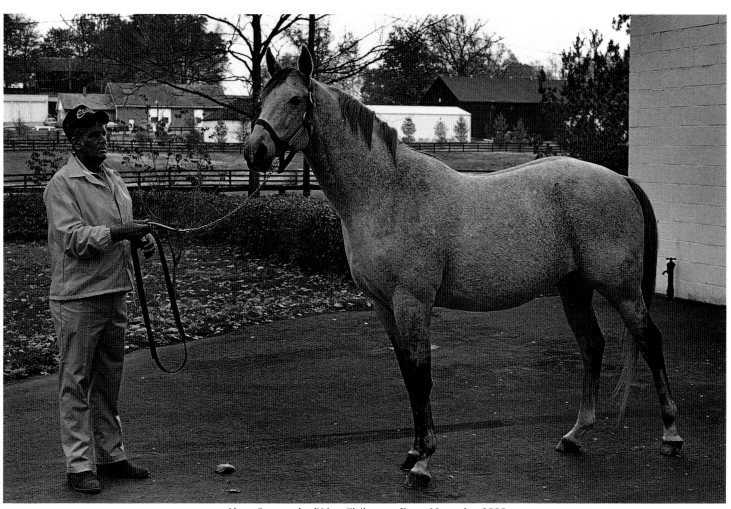

*Above*: Spectacular Bid at Claibourne Farm, November 1988

*Below*: Secretariat at Claibourne Farm, November 1988

*Above*: The parterre boxes

# MONMOUTH PARK

OCEANPORT, NEW JERSEY

There have been three Monmouth Park racetracks. The first one, built in 1870, was the largest racetrack in the country: located on 660 acres, it had an iron grandstand 1,100 feet long, a paddock with ninety-six stalls, and a 1¾-mile track. Between 1891 and 1941, anti-racing legislation in New Jersey eliminated the sport, but after it was legalized, Garden State Park in Cherry Hill and Atlantic City were the first to build new tracks. Although the racing commission approved a track at Monmouth, it took five years to sell shares and raise the 3.5 million dollars needed to construct the new Monmouth Park, which opened in June 1946. The project was developed largely by Amory Haskell and a group of men interested in horse sports—hunting, jumping, showing, and racing. While Haskell was president of the Monmouth Park Jockey Club, Philip Iselin became interested in the park, originally because it bordered his property, and was appointed treasurer, and Edward J. Brennan acted as general manager. In the early years this was considered to be a resort racetrack for people who went to the New Jersey shore in July and August and did not want to travel to Belmont and Saratoga. It is now a suburban track whose patrons are local year-round residents.

Monmouth Park was built, as were all early racetracks, with separate grandstand and clubhouse structures divided by a horse path leading from the paddock to the racetrack. The clubhouse had five stories, which racetrack publicity of the period described as "the most amazing structure on American turf," and had two tiers of parterre boxes, which were copied at Keeneland in 1990. Each box has a private dining area for six people at the back and chairs in the front to view the races. The parterre boxes were so successful that a third tier was added.

The main characteristic of the Monmouth buildings is openness, a result of pre-air-conditioning design and the seashore location. Mesh-wire sectionals divide the betting and receiving areas in the grandstand. Balconies overlook the paddock area and were completely open when the clubhouse and grandstand were built, but horizontal sliding-glass windows were later installed to keep out winter weather. There were seven outdoor dining terraces in the clubhouse when the building opened in 1946, and although several remain, they are enclosed in glass partitions that look as though they are rarely opened. At the core of the clubhouse is a formal but comfortable lounge, which is located off a hallway behind the boxes. The interior decoration has been maintained from the 1940s, most notably the black-and-white tile floors, gilded birdcages, rattan furniture, chintz slipcovers, wallpaper, and paintings. "We always had a decorator," says Mrs. Philip Iselin. "My husband wanted it to look like a country place."

The architect of the buildings was Mark Linenthal of Boston, who, before Arthur Froehlich began designing racetracks, was probably the leading American architect of such facilities. He founded his firm in 1921 after graduating from Harvard and was a structural engineer who either designed or consulted on many tracks: Suffolk Downs and Rockingham Park in the 1930s, Monmouth Park and a track in Las Vegas in the 1940s, the clubhouse at Pimlico in the 1950s, and a grandstand building at Oaklawn in 1957. Most of the firm's work consisted of single buildings or projects such as enclosing grandstands with glass windows. L. Rex Anderson, who joined the firm in 1954, says that Linenthal also designed a dog track, Raynham, near Providence, Rhode Island, and became part owner when he couldn't collect his fee, a deal that ultimately brought him more income than did his engineering firm. His connection with racing comes from his close friendship with Louis Smith, who became the owner of Rockingham Park in 1931 and who introduced him to other clients such as Amory Haskell at Monmouth Park and John Cella at Oaklawn. The early grandstand seated 2,800 and had two observation towers overlooking the paddock, which were later removed. The section between the clubhouse and grandstand was filled in and the grandstand expanded in the 1960s by Arthur Froehlich & Associates, which resulted in a facility that can seat about 20,000 people. A separate, two-story house was built in 1945 near the main entrance. Resembling a gatehouse, it houses the administration offices, director's room, and library. In 1988 a new saddling shed was built in the area between the administration building and the jockeys' quarters.

The pride of the racetrack, however, is the small walking ring with its small grassy area in the center and four birch trees. It is surrounded by a wide path of wood chips and is edged with a gooseneck railing filled in by boxwood hedges. Because of this fence, similar to the one at Ascot, the walking ring at Monmouth is referred to as an English walking ring.

*Right*: The boxes and grandstand apron

*Above*: The grandstand from the far turn

*Below*: The post parade before the race

*Above*: Spiral hedge in the infield designed by A.F. Brinkerhauf

*Above*: View from the clubhouse restaurant

*Above*: The clubhouse lounge

*Below*: The clubhouse hallway

*Above*: The center of the walking ring

*Below*: The Horseman's Path, or gap, from the track to the paddock

*Right*: Walking ring from the public viewing area

*Above*: Trompe l'oeil lattice in the clubhouse entrance hall

*Above*: Main betting hall in the grandstand

*Below*: The back of the grandstand

*Above*: Terrace of owner's house at the edge of the main course

# OAKLAWN PARK

HOT SPRINGS, ARKANSAS

In 1918 racetrack holdings ascribed to the Cella family of St. Louis, Missouri, were recorded in various racing publications as City Park in New Orleans; Latonia near Cincinnati; Douglas Park in Louisville; Fort Erie near Buffalo; Del Mar Park, Kinloch, and the St. Louis Fair Grounds in St. Louis; Oaklawn Park in Hot Springs; Highlands Park in Detroit; Cumberland Park in Nashville; and Montgomery Park in Memphis. The racetracks were acquired by Louis Cella and his brother Charles in the early years of the century, and although some of the tracks closed due to the anti-racing sentiment that prevailed until the 1930s, they were exceptional as large pieces of urban real estate in the years to come.

Oaklawn Park started to function as a major track in 1934, thirty years after it opened. The racetrack at Hot Springs, which opened in 1904, was closed in 1907 when Arkansas declared wagering on horse racing illegal. It was revived by the city in 1916, then closed again in 1919 to reopen in 1934, when the Business Men's Racing Association decided to support racing at Oaklawn in order to generate business. The mayor and leading businessmen sanctioned "spa racing," and the state passed legislation permitting parimutuel wagering the following year.

The track was managed by Louis Cella's brother, Charles, throughout those years when the track was being reformed. For owners of horses who did not go to Florida, Oaklawn became an important place for winter racing. With racing dates from February to April, it provided an opportunity to run horses before the opening of Keeneland in April, Churchill Downs for the Kentucky Derby in May, and Arlington Park in Chicago in the summer. The Arkansas Derby, for three-year-old horses, was instituted as a stakes race in 1935.

In 1941 Charles Cella died and his son John inherited Oaklawn Park. He also inherited the racetrack at Fort Erie, but sold it in order to concentrate on Oaklawn. John Cella's method of management was described in his obituary in *The Blood-Horse*, October 19, 1968: "He relied entirely for the actual operations on the track and racing officials he engaged, but mixed with horsemen on the backstretch and with track employees engaged in various duties, then circulated among patrons during the afternoon racing, thus exercising close supervision while seeking additional ways to improve the plant and the general operation." In 1942 John Cella made Oaklawn Park a charter member of the Thoroughbred Racing Association, an organization founded in order to legitimize and promote racing. He chose to live at the racetrack during the racing season, in a ranch-style house he built at the edge of the racing strip opposite the ⅛-mile pole. This combination of seriousness, team

*Above*: The finishing line

management, and a somewhat theatrical manner of living seems to have been adopted by his son, Charles, who assumed ownership of Oaklawn Park after John's death in 1968. He sold a sizable portion of stock in the racetrack in 1970, but repurchased the shares within a year. There was a substantial increase in attendance in the 1970s, when Charles introduced new and expanded stakes races.

The architecture and landscaping at Oaklawn is a patchwork, the product of various expansion programs which took place over the years. The racetrack is located in an area bounded by residential and commercial neighborhoods, allowing for very little parking space and virtually no expansion. There is no master plan that hinders or aids the development of this track, but it does seem to embody the caprices of its owner.

There are three grandstand buildings, constructed in 1959, 1973 and 1976, which replace portions of the 1904 buildings, and a new log house erected in 1987 along the homestretch. The 1959 building, designed by the engineering firm of Linenthal & Becker, Boston, replaces a 1904 enclosed paddock with a glass-and-cement grandstand (which includes a paddock room with a mezzanine for viewing the horses). Mark Linenthal had designed various racetrack buildings in the Northeast prior to Oaklawn, most prominent among them Suffolk Downs, Rockingham Park, and Monmouth Park. The building is dressed in a local sandstone and was characterized by a facade of English-made, metal-

*Above*: The infield once a golfcourse

encased windows that swing upward, which were replaced in 1990. The 1959 building joined a very pretty 1904 wooden grandstand with Queen Anne-style detailing. In 1973 a major grandstand was added (Engineering Consultants, Little Rock, Arkansas; Lee Bransford, project architect), which had thick glass walls with glass fins—a product by Libby, Owens, Ford called Total Vision System. In 1976 the little 1904 grandstand was replaced with a structure with vertical mullions and glass by Arthur Froehlich & Associates, Beverly Hills, and Morio Kow, design architect. In 1983 the final strips of glass were put in the face of the now greatly expanded set of buildings, filling in the 1953–69 addition. (A northern wing was built in 1953 to provide more seating, and two bays were added in 1969 by the Little Rock firm of Erhart Eichenbaum Raugh and Blass. Stadium seating, brought from Rice University in Houston, was added in front so that fans could enjoy the outside breezes instead of air conditioning or heat behind the now immovable glass.)

Nothing remains of the 1904 grandstand. Photographs of it show that dormers were placed at intervals around the hipped roof and there was a large cupola. The dormers were not simply decorative but were used as small press boxes holding two or three reporters each. All sides of this rather formal grandstand building had large sash windows, like those at the stand at the Fair Grounds in New Orleans. It was steam-heated and the sashes could be fully opened during fair weather. Henry Schrader, the contractor, was entrusted by the

169

earliest owners—the Cellas, John Condon, Dan Stuart, and C.B. Dugan—to build the racetrack with forty men and $500,000. A separate, two-story paddock building, also completely enclosed, was connected to the grandstand on the second level by a bridge, and patrons could view the horses from above. In the present paddock, located in the ground floor of the grandstand building erected in 1959, the ceiling is very low and the crowds view the horses from a slightly elevated level, but without the benefit of the sunlight that streamed through the two stories of glass in the earlier building.

The infield landscaping is a patchwork as well, consisting of what was once a nine-hole golf course at the earlier racetrack. The infield plantings of juniper trees are remnants of the course, as is the rolling terrain. There are some odd contradictions, including a large area of dark aqua-painted concrete amid natural grass, and an elliptical temple designed by Charles Cella as a memorial to his favorite dog. There is an English gazebo made of fiberglass, and a large, digital tote board behind the name of Oaklawn written in boxwood hedges. The

*Above*: The main entrance

winner's circle is located in the infield within a horseshoe fence of boxwood. A large bronze statue of racing horses stands in a rose garden directly behind the circle. The golf course was eliminated by 1973, when a tunnel to the infield was constructed and a small crab apple orchard was planted to create a picnic area. The present infield is open to the fans on weekends during the main racing week at the end of April. During the final racing days in April, before stakes races, the horses are saddled in the infield on a strip of grass edged by blossoming apple trees. The remaining portion is enclosed by a white fence formerly used to pasture the horses and mules that pulled the harrows (light plows that smooth the soil) and the Clydesdale team that pulled the starting gate into place before each race.

*Above*: The grandstand

*Below*: View of the grandstand and owner's house from the backstretch

*Overleaf*: The maintenance barn

*Above*: A "Cottage" barn

In 1987 Charles Cella replaced his father's house at the ⅛-mile pole with a kit log house—he is the owner of the Michigan company that produces these kit houses—and replaced the backstretch kitchen with a similar structure. The backstretch contains a greater variety of barns than does any other place in racing. The oldest barns, of which there are nine, are referred to as cottage barns and are handsome structures with stalls for horses on the ground floor, a hay room, a tack room, and upstairs living quarters. They were built when the racetrack was founded in 1904. Five other barns are long, shed-row stalls, with an aisle in the middle allowing them to be twice the normal length, and have an area for hay storage upstairs. There is a two-story, Federal-style house on each end to provide living quarters. These have brick facades, but at least one of these barns is sided in horizontal tongue-and-groove wood paneling covered in brick. These are referred to as original barns, but are said to date from the 1950s. Until recently, an entire section of barns called Silver City was located behind the fence along Central Avenue. They had been covered in silver paint and lended to the patchwork quality of the place, but were demolished in the 1980s to make room for a parking lot. A group of nine new barns was erected in 1981, based on the fireproof masonry block barns at Keeneland and replacing the stall space provided by Silver City. These barns were given the names of horses instead of the numbers that designate the early barns. Later, a landfill was used to erect seven duplicate barns. The main streets of the

174

*Above*: Shed row and "Cottage" barns

stable area were paved. All this construction was under the direction of General Manager W.T. Bishop, who had been an important figure in the development of Keeneland Race Course from 1936 until 1972.

During the 1930s, the leading stable was owned by Emil Denemark, owner of the Cadillac dealership in Chicago, who had constructed one of the shed-row barns on the backstretch, renamed for the racehorse Count Fleet in 1981. Denemark's son-in-law was Al Capone, who frequented the Arlington Hotel (though apparently not the racetrack), located at the other end of Central Avenue in the area of the thermal springs and bathhouses. Capone and his men would take a floor of the hotel when they were avoiding Chicago. During the 1930s the Hot Springs city administration tolerated casinos and the police allowed visitors to the resort; only Federal authorities made the occasional arrest there. Now the central portion of the city is a national park, the baths are museums, the casinos are closed, and the racetrack is one of the city's biggest tourist industries.

*Above*: Backstretch kitchen and shed row barns

*Right*: The bridle path and new barns  *Overleaf*: Shed row of a "Cottage" barn

*Above*: Trainer D. Wayne Lukas (center) at The Arkansas Derby

*Above*: The Arkansas Derby, April 22, 1989

*Right*: Mr. Billy's Tip City on Central Avenue

# MR. BILLY'S
# TIP CITY
## LEADING TIP SHEET • NOT SOLD IN TRACK

# "THE OFFICE"
## TIP SHEET STORE #3

REDEEM COUPON HERE

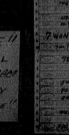

FREE!! OFFICIAL PROGRAM WITH ANY PURCHASE!!

REDEEM COUPON HERE

*Above*: Shed row

*Below*: The living quarters of Barn No. 26

*Right*: Dogwood tree in the infield

*Above*: Oaklawn President Charles Cella

*Below*: Needlepoint footstool in Charles Cella's house

*Above*: Handicappers' seminar at the Arlington Hotel in downtown Hot Springs

*Below:* Dining room in Charles Cella's house

*Above*: Jockeys' quarters and silks room

*Right*: Saddle pads drying

# SANTA ANITA PARK

The idea for a new racetrack in southern California came from film producer and director Hal Roach and was organized by Gwynn Wilson and Dr. Charles Strub, who were affiliated with amateur and professional sports. The money to develop the project was raised in both Hollywood and San Francisco in 1933, after the state of California voted to reinstate racing. Roach, who brought to the American public Laurel and Hardy, Harold Lloyd, and Will Rogers, organized the project and located the initial money. He assembled a group of friends and associates in Hollywood who were interested in creating a racetrack and, at the suggestion of one of them, brought in Wilson to develop and manage the project. Wilson had just completed his role as Associate General Manager of the 1932 Los Angeles Olympics and was a highly visible figure in California. The next step was to raise a million dollars, a figure established by the state as the amount necessary before a license could be granted. Roach and Wilson were able to raise $500,000, most of it from people in the film business, but were unable to raise more. They approached every person they knew in Los Angeles, and Wilson says that "by the end of November people would no longer talk to me when they saw me coming down the street." He heard about Dr. Strub, in San Francisco, who had the necessary backing but was having difficulty getting the city to give him approval to build a racetrack. Strub left San Francisco and joined the group and, by all accounts, everything fell into place after he arrived. "Dr. Strub was the dominant person in terms of the direction," says Wilson. "He brought in the top money. We had $500,000 in cash, and that's all. He came in and brought the rest. He was the spark." Strub brought $350,000 from San Francisco and put up $150,000, for which he was reimbursed in stock the following year. Strub, one of three owners of the San Francisco Seals, a minor-league baseball team, took over the racing end of the project. His son, Robert Strub, the current president of Santa Anita Park, says that his father made being the head of the racetrack the condition on which he agreed to leave San Francisco and relocate in Los Angeles.

In January 1934, the Los Angeles Turf Club was incorporated; Hal Roach was President, Charles Strub was Executive Vice President, and Gwynn Wilson assumed the role of Assistant General Manager. Strub and Wilson kept offices at the racetrack and were the heart of its administration for the next twenty-five years. Their jobs were always equal—one ran racing and the other managed the plant. Wilson recalls: "Hal Roach was very easy to get along with, made his money in comedy, and was very funny himself. His idea was to have a lot of tents, somewhere at the beach, so I selected the architect."

189

The designer was Gordon B. Kaufmann, a society architect, who had built several prestigious houses in La Quinta and Bel Air in period revival styles. This is precisely why he was chosen, since historic references implied not only a sound establishment, but also heritage and good taste. Furthermore, since racing had been outlawed in California for twenty-five years, the new facility had to inspire confidence and respectability. Wilson says that there were only two major architects in Los Angeles at the time, John Parkinson and Gordon Kaufmann. Wilson knew Parkinson better and had worked with him during the construction of the Student Union at the University of Southern California, where Wilson was the athletic director, and again during the construction of Los Angeles's Olympic Stadium. But Kaufmann was the right choice for the track. Architectural historian David Gebhard writes that period revival architecture had been "an ingredient of L.A. since the days of Mission Revival in the early 1900s. By the late 1930s it had discarded its earlier historic garments and fully embraced the Moderne." This racetrack, to be successful in a slightly hostile environment, needed to be both conservative and modern.

Neither Wilson nor Kaufmann had ever been to a racetrack, so they left immediately on an odyssey to look at facilities across the country. They travelled by plane, which Wilson says was "like a barn with wings that shook and had lots of ventilation," to Abilene, continuing by train to a few tracks which Wilson describes as "rough and not our conception of a racetrack at all." They reached New Orleans at Mardi Gras and visited the Fair Grounds but "didn't learn anything." From there they went to Hialeah and immediately realized that it was what they wanted, "a resort type of a racetrack, more for recreation than for strictly gambling." They studied the buildings and the track; Kaufmann made notes and sketches while Wilson took measurements. Both knew that they needed a facility with a larger and less restricted clubhouse. They continued north to Maryland and New York, looking at the old tracks at Pimlico and Belmont. At Arlington Park outside Chicago they found another modern racetrack that interested them. "Arlington and Hialeah are the basis from which we started," says Wilson, who recalls that they talked racetracks twenty-four hours a day for the three weeks of the trip, and that they knew what they wanted by the end. They took an airplane from Chicago to Phoenix, and a train from Phoenix to Los Angeles. Wilson remembers this trip affectionately, saying "Nobody knew Gordon better than I did after that."

Kaufmann spent thirty days preparing the drawings and Strub selected contractors from Pasadena and Los Angeles, choosing Lindgren & Swinerton as the builders. They started building within three weeks after Wilson and Kaufmann returned from their trip, beginning with extensive grading of the site and preparation of the track. Santa Anita, like Hialeah, was built in a short span of time, about seven months, and employed twenty-eight different general contracting firms.

The site of the racetrack is at the foot of the San Gabriel Mountains, a range of handsome, bare, sometimes snow-capped mountains that rise up just beyond the backstretch. As the light varies throughout the day, the mountains appear to change color. Majestic is a fair description of the location, and the June 1937 issue of *Architectural Forum*

*Above*: The paddock

*Overleaf*: The paddock

called it unsurpassed. Roach had been interested in making the racetrack more accessible by locating it closer to downtown Los Angeles, but was persuaded to build at the historic and beautiful location of Arcadia. An earlier racetrack had been built there by Elias Jackson "Lucky" Baldwin within an enormous tract of land called Rancho Santa Anita.

Baldwin was one of two people who pioneered the breeding of Thoroughbred horses in California. He began shipping his California-bred horses east in 1885, winning seven stakes races. One of the Baldwin silks (the colored shirts worn by the jockey identifying the stable for which he rides), black with a Maltese Cross, is in a glass case in the Director's Room at the Turf Club. The remains of his four American Derby-winning horses lie under a Maltese Cross statue at the eastern end of the paddock, moved from his nearby racetrack. He built hotels and a casino to supplement his racetrack, making it more attractive for patrons to journey out to Arcadia. Racing was banned in California in 1909, two years after he opened the track. By 1934 Baldwin's track was an artifact, an oval outline in the dirt located on land adjacent to the new Santa Anita Park.

Kaufmann drew a large parking lot into his plans; his scheme is one of the earliest complexes to include elaborate provisions for automobiles. The "unsurpassed location" also refers to the accessibility of the track, which can be reached easily from all four directions: Pasadena from the north and west, Los Angeles from the south, and Arcadia and San Bernardino from the west. Two long, palm-lined drives lead from Huntington Avenue on the east and southeast to the clubhouse, which offers valet parking. The 10,000-car parking lot is convenient to the paddock and the main entrance. In 1934 the average daily attendance was 9,000, but that had doubled by 1937. Another parking lot was added on the north side of the racetrack, allowing patrons to easily reach the infield via a tunnel. A wide walkway runs across the infield to a tunnel leading into the grandstand and the paddock. Kaufmann wrote that circulation was the essence of good racetrack design, encouraging great numbers of people to congregate on a relatively small area of the homestretch, and to move quickly to restaurants, refreshment stands, betting areas, service areas, infield, paddock, and the parking lots. Betting rooms run the full length of the grandstand and are open on the front so that crowds can enter from the track or the paddock. He designed a grandstand that seated 6,000, making provisions for its extension and for an increase in the size of the clubhouse. In 1935, at the end of the first season, bleachers were built which were eventually enclosed and incorporated into the grandstand; eighty elevated boxes were added to the clubhouse; and a tunnel was constructed to the infield.

Racetracks are a little like old-fashioned ocean liners in that they are divided into classes; besides the general-admission grandstand facilities, Santa Anita has a clubhouse with lounges, restaurants, and a betting room, and a Turf Club composed of the same set of rooms, although they are completely private: the Director's Room, the Americana Room, the Brazilian Room dining area, and the Lanai Room. In 1937, the two clubhouses could accommodate 5,000 people. A fourth class has recently been added for corporate patrons, housed in a new area called the Clubhouse Terrace. Other new additions include a tent enclosing a statue of Seabiscuit in the paddock area and various pavilions in the infield. The

*Above*: The Turf Club

racetrack now comfortably holds 50,000 spectators.

Kaufmann's clubhouse facade is not unlike the private residences he designed; it is a modern Georgian mansion with a tall, central portico supported by very slender, paired columns. An arched doorway is reached by semicircular steps and white plaster urns decorate the cornice. The back of the clubhouse portion of the grandstand, also facing east, includes Georgian detailing and is set back from the clubhouse entrance. A recent addition with Hollywood Regency detailing covers this building. The clubhouse and main grandstand were at one time separated by the horse chute or pathway between the grandstand and clubhouse. This pathway existed at all early tracks and is called the gap, which originally meant the gap between the two buildings. In the original design, a bridge spans the gap and links the grandstand to the loge seating of the clubhouse. All the buildings are of steel and concrete with a plaster surface painted blue-green to reduce the glare. Apparently, Kaufmann fulfilled his obligation to his clients with his clubhouse design, because a contemporary account suggests that it was "Inspired perhaps by the heritage of the Kentucky Derby, its Colonial entrance might very well grace an old Southern mansion."

However, the grandstand is pure 1930s Los Angeles in terms of style and decoration. The back of the grandstand is covered with a series of shallow bays, alternatively covered by two decorative panels and two louvered panels, each about six feet high and fifty feet wide. The panels depict a stylized version of a race from wire to wire, since the grandstand is at the beginning and the end with the turns suggested in between. They are punched out of sheet steel and are backed with glass, now painted over. There is a main entrance in this facade (although none is necessary since once within the gates one can enter anywhere), which is tall, white, and topped with flags. The cost of building the racetrack was $850,000, the land $200,000, and Wilson recalls that Kaufmann's design fee was $5,000 in secured stock. After designing Santa Anita Park, Kaufmann's work included the Earl Carroll Theater, The Los Angeles Times Building, and the monumental Art Deco structure, Boulder (Hoover) Dam. The structural engineer for Santa Anita was Paul Jeffers, author of California's first, and current, earthquake code.

The paddock and infield are the work of landscape architect Tommy Tomson, who was hired by Kaufmann. The paddock, based on a formal garden, had an oval walking ring at the center and is approached by eight walkways planted with boxwood hedges, topiary, and highly decorative trees. Tomson discovered these fine, full-grown Brazilian pepper trees in the town of Inglewood (available because they were insect-infested, a condition he knew how to treat), and had them moved to Santa Anita. Low wooden fences that roll on casters protect the spectators while the horses enter the walking circle. The fences are quickly rolled back after the horses proceed to the track, leaving the entire area free to cross. The statuary urns and column in the center of the walking circle were brought from England in the 1950s by Strub. The building housing the jockeys' quarters and the saddling shed was built in 1950; it replaces a curved building designed by Kaufmann which was located between the stables and the paddock.

The paddock is such an unusual and spectacular place, especially when viewed from

*Above*: The Turf Club

*Below*: The Regency Room

above, that stock footage of it was included in nearly every movie made about racing for a decade after its completion. The Marx Brothers filmed *A Day At The Races* at Santa Anita in 1937. Featured at the end of the film are views of the grandstand, the bridge over the gap, paddock, infield, and stable areas, all of which confirm how little Santa Anita has changed over the years. That the racetrack has retained a coherent visual image is a feat, since there have been constant changes and at least four architects who have worked on Santa Anita since it was built. As Wilson says, "You can't take Kaufmann out of the racetrack. The basics out there are Kaufmann's and you can't hide them. He is there."

Santa Anita is the only racetrack that uses its infield every day. Tomson originally planted its thirty-four acres almost solidly with flowers to form decorative patterns, using "hundreds of thousands of yellow and orange calendulas, ruby violas, blue and white pansies, and primulas." Apparently the design changed annually. A 1939 photograph shows the infield planted with a giant formal grid reflecting the shapes in the paddock garden; a picture dated 1940 shows plantings shaped like the wings of a butterfly. In a Warner Brothers film, *The Story of Seabiscuit*, with Shirley Temple and a very good interpretation of a horse owner's wife by Rosemary DeCamp, actual footage of a race is used, which shows the infield planted entirely with golden flowers. Tomson's career lasted over fifty years; he also laid out the town of Palm Desert. Currently the infield is composed of a variety of playgrounds, refreshment stands, and pavilions landscaped with palm trees in islands of English ivy and fountains. Mariachi bands stroll on the main walkway, playing music before the races. The infield provides space for people to relax, play with their children, and get away from the noise of the crowd. Even on the biggest racing day it is possible to find a fairly quiet place on the infield. The average daily attendance is around 30,000, and statistics show that attendance has not varied significantly since 1945. On March 7, 1947, a record attendance was set at 83,768; the current record was established on March 6, 1985, when 85,527 people came to the track. A fairly normal major day attendance is 65,000.

At Santa Anita, horses are both the main event and the opening acts. Patrol judges, who sit in towers placed at intervals around the track (to monitor interference during the racing), ride there in two hackneys drawn by teams of two and four standardbred horses, whose drivers wear tall, black silk hats and coats with tails. From 5:00 to 7:00 A.M. the track is used to exercise and clock the horses. These morning workouts are especially colorful because the ponies (this name refers to all horses other than Thoroughbreds) are frequently Western-bred, spotted horses that provide a visual relief from the sleek, solid-hued Thoroughbreds. Furthermore, their riders wear leather chaps and Western hats. In the early days, the track owned teams of Belgiums, a breed of workhorses, to draw the harrows that smoothed the track surface, a task now carried out quickly by tractors. The starting gate was pulled into place by these teams until the 1970s, and in the 1980s a famous team of Clydesdales was contracted by the racetrack to perform the job.

Wilson sums up: "My contribution was the recreation. We knew that racetrackers will come, but if you include recreation more people will come, relax. You've got to have beauty and you've got to have comfort. You have to provide a facility to show the elegance of the

*Above*: Foyer of The Regency Room

*Below*: The Americana Room

sport. Recreation, creature comforts, and you've got to have confidence in racing. I think that Willie Shoemaker contributed as much to racing as anyone. Everyone has confidence in Willie because he has character. Willie and Whittingham, the two of them together have created a sort or relationship between the public and the participants in racing that is a little closer than it usually is." William Shoemaker, one of the world's greatest jockeys from 1949 to 1989, is now a trainer. Charles Whittingham has been a trainer at Santa Anita from 1934 to the present. Both established national records in their fields.

In 1935 Roach and Strub introduced the concept of having a stakes race with $100,000 added, thereby creating the richest race in history. Even though it was the Depression and the racetrack was new and unknown, Roach and Strub had the confidence that comes with backgrounds in show business and sports entertainment. The purse of a stakes race is the total of the nomination fees collected from the owners of horses entered in the race, plus the guarantee added by the track, which is then divided among the first four finishers. The addition of $100,000 was not only good advertising, but it was an enticement for prominent Eastern racing families to ship their horses to California for the race. With the $100,000 Santa Anita Handicap on February 23, 1935, the importance and prominence of Santa Anita Park was established. In 1986 the Santa Anita Handicap became the world's first stakes race with one million dollars added.

Strub also introduced a beautifully conceived turf course in 1953. The course starts on a hillside northwest of the track oval and proceeds southward and downhill for three-quarters of a mile with the Botanical Gardens as a backdrop. It swoops into a curve near the barns and proceeds across the dirt track and onto a turf course which runs inside the dirt track oval. The race is 1¾ miles with a six-furlong start. It is often described as a European-style course, which probably refers to the fact that the horses are initially out of sight and that the course is irregular. This extremely handsome course is called the Camino Real and, not surprisingly, a $100,000 stakes race was introduced during its first season on March 6, 1954. Known as the San Juan Capistrano Handicap, it is the first stakes race on grass of that magnitude.

During the rest of 1930s there were several referendums in California against racing that were defeated, and Thoroughbred racing soon emerged as an acceptable sport. The sport of kings in Southern California was the sport of motion-picture moguls. In 1937 Del Mar, near San Diego, was constructed and presided over by Bing Crosby, and in 1938 the Hollywood Park racetrack was built in Inglewood with financial backing from Warner Brothers, both of which further confirmed the public's acceptance of racing and the state's interest in its revenues.

This world of generated income, entertainment, fast horses, and sleek architecture was radically changed with the bombing of Pearl Harbor; the entire facility of Santa Anita was confiscated. According to Wilson, "Everything was ready. The horses were in the barns, the flowers were in their beds, all we had to do was just ring the bell. Then came December 7th, and all was shot down. Within a week they came and took it over and made an

internment camp there. The horses had to go back to the farms. The government told the horsemen to get out. We were ready to go and the rest of the racetracks were dead at that time. They could have picked Hollywood Park." From December 1941 until 1944, the racetrack was the site of one of the most tragic decisions in American history—the internment of Japanese-Americans in detention camps for the entire duration of the Second World War. Barracks were erected in the parking lots and the infield, the barns were used as living space, and the grandstand was used as classroom area. Wilson and Strub arranged for the paddock and the Turf Club to be kept off-limits, and when the government relocated the camp they gave the Los Angeles Turf Club one million dollars to restore the facility. According to Wilson, "They went in roughshod and did a pretty good job of tearing it down. It was hard, but there was no damage done that couldn't be put back together." Racing resumed in 1945.

*Above*: The clubhouse loggia

*Above and Overleaf:* Ticket booth below loggia

*Above*: Urn and horse topiary in the paddock

*Above*: View of the grandstand from the Kingsbury Fountain

*Below*: The Paddock Room

*Overleaf*: View of the backstretch and the San Gabriel Mountains

*Above*: Track announcer Trevor Denman

*Above*: Racing secretary Jimmy Kilroe

*Above*: Santa Anita President Robert Strub

*Above*: Track patrons

*Above*: The Turf Club entrance walk

*Right*: The main entrance and gates

*Above*: The clubhouse entrance

*Above*: Morning workout

*Below*: The Camino Real turf course with a view of the Botanical Gardens

*Overleaf*: Opening day ceremony

*Above*: The barn area

*Below:* The saddling shed

*Right*: Sign at Huntington Avenue entrance

PUBLIC
INVITED
TO
MORNING
WORKOUTS
DAILY 7:30 A.M. to 9:30 A.M.
Stable
Tours
SATURDAY
AND
SUNDAY

# SARATOGA RACE COURSE

Saratoga Race Course is the oldest racetrack in America, dating from 1864. The area in front of the grandstand, known as the infield at every other track, is curiously referred to as the front yard by the grounds crew. Likewise, the area behind it is called the backyard, implying that the grandstand is the big house. The present clubhouse and grandstand are a quarter of a mile long, but at the nucleus is a building erected in 1892 whose roof is graced with a bouquet of turrets. This little grandstand building has a powerful presence. It measures about 585 feet and is constructed of wood posts and beams. Wood trusses support a slate-shingle roof with three towers at the center and a single turret at each end. It fills the skyline with sweeping diagonal planes. Each of the pinnacles along the roof is sheathed in a gilded crocket—an ornamentation that architectural historian Norval White defines as a teat on a Gothic finial. This heavy, yet sensual, silhouette has long remained the dominant feature of the racetrack, even when subsequent structures enveloped it.

This part of the grandstand contains the best boxes, which are spare enclosures made of tongue-and-groove paneling that contain bentwood chairs for the wealthy owners and breeders—A-28 belongs to Ogden Phipps, B-28 to The King Ranch, A-30 to the Governor, A-31 to John Von Staade, A-32 to Mrs. John A. Morris, A-33 to Alfred Vanderbilt, and A-27 to James Brady. The less prestigious boxes further up the homestretch contain slightly more comfortable chairs, made of nylon webbing and aluminum tubing. Ceiling fans hang from the trusses, but the patrons are primarily cooled by the shade of the roof and the wind that rustles the tall pines behind the grandstand.

An octagonal tower is attached to the grandstand located directly on the finish line. It has an overhang which gives the best view of the finish to the three placing judges; below them are the stewards. Three buildings—the central part of the grandstand, the saddling shed located in the paddock behind the clubhouse, and the now-demolished betting ring— were constructed between 1891 and 1902. There is a medieval feeling to these buildings, evoking a castle, kings, and men on horseback. The movie *Saratoga*, filmed at the racetrack in 1937, gives a sense of the mass of these buildings, albeit briefly; the buildings also serve as a backdrop for the portraits of late nineteenth-century horse patrons such as Lillian Russell and Diamond Jim Brady in the famous Cook photographic archive in the library at

*Left*: Decorative ironwork on clubhouse porch   *Overleaf*: Horses being led to the paddock

*Above*: The grandstand from the far turn

Keeneland. These shingle-style buildings are firmly anchored to the landscape, straightforward in construction, and full of variety. The clubhouse, on the other hand, is light, airy, graceful, large in scale, and has a wealth of Beaux-Arts detailing. Saratoga Race Course, in terms of its architectural references, is the best of both worlds.

The clubhouse, completed by 1941, is largely the work of Albany architect Kenneth Reynolds, whose Saratoga projects include the Gideon Putnam Hotel and the harness-racing track. His father, Marcus Reynolds, a student at the Ecole des Beaux-Arts, produced buildings with this flair throughout the 1920s. The rear section of the clubhouse, facing the paddock, has wrought-iron posts with horse-head braces holding up a curved roof that is sheathed in copper and scalloped at the edge. This section is enclosed by a picket fence. The former clubhouse entrance (converted in the 1970s into the Travers Bar) has an elliptical portico with six horse-head posts supporting a lintel that is decorated with scalloped carpentry and carved horse heads. A wide overhang supports flower boxes. Two rows of fluted Doric columns make a little temple entrance to the dining area, which is often used for early breakfasts. Until recently the tables were located on both sides of the path between the paddock and the track, so that the horses and jockeys walked between the diners. Now the gap is located just outside the clubhouse entrance; you can still see the horses and jockeys from the tables, but the easy accessibility to the horse and rider has been eliminated.

226

*Right*: The finishing line and tower

The oval saddling shed surrounds the stalls in which horses were saddled and paraded on rainy days until 1963, when the stalls were enclosed to create outdoor parimutuel windows. There is a clean expanse of roof, covered in slate shingles with the low overhang intact. The long roof is pierced by triangular dormer windows to light the dark interior. The shed must have been an exquisite pavilion when it was still used for saddling.

Next to the grandstand was a highly unusual building, now demolished, called the betting ring. It was almost as large as the saddling shed, rectangular in shape with a hipped, shingle roof that was low at the eaves and rose as tall as the grandstand. Several bookmakers had their headquarters in this building. Mark Costello, a former resident manager at Saratoga and an architectural draftsman, remembers eight bookmakers in the 1950s, each of whom had a slate man to write up the bets.

In 1902, after W.C. Whitney had acquired the track, he had the grandstand, betting ring, and field stand moved 400 feet to align with a newly constructed racing course. There have been no major changes since that time. The July 25, 1902, issue of *Turf, Field and Farm* describes the new track and new saddling shed (250 by 72 feet) as the work of civil and landscape engineer Charles W. Leavitt, Jr. of New York, who also built the Empire Track at Yonkers, and his assistant engineer W. E. Spinner. The *Thoroughbred Record* of July 1902, describes the reconstruction of the betting ring (175 by 90 feet) as having a "monitor" placed in the roof for more light and air. This building, located to the east of the grandstand, along with the field stand next to it, was demolished in 1963 in order to construct the present grandstand extension. This new grandstand portion was designed by the Beverly Hills firm of Arthur Froehlich, with Robert Krause as design architect. There is a continuity of materials, and small turrets define both ends. All subsequent architectural work at Saratoga—the development of the Carousel wing, and the construction of a new parimutuel pavilion in 1984 and a restroom facility in 1987—has been designed by Krause, of Ewing Cole Cherry Parsky.

Another large grandstand, called the field stand, was built in 1892. Every racetrack had a similar stand located on the stretch farthest away from the clubhouse. Although the stated intention of these stands was to charge a lower admission, in actuality these grandstands were used by the many African-American jockeys, trainers, grooms, stable hands, and track patrons in the early years of American Thoroughbred racing. In nearly all cases, they were demolished in the 1960s during the height of the civil rights movement. The black stand at Saratoga was built sometime in the nineteenth century and was demolished in 1963 along with the betting ring in order to extend the grandstand; the black stands were demolished at Keeneland in 1955 and at the Fair Grounds by the 1970s for the same reason. The concrete foundation of the black stand at Hialeah still exists, although there were several lower-admission stands at that particular track.

On the backstretch at Saratoga, across Union Avenue, was a recreation center with segregated swimming pools, eating facilities, barber shops, and Ping-Pong areas. Located in a separate building was a boxing arena, in which individual stables would put up the best fighters among their employees, and the events were a major part of the season. These

*Above*: The Carousel Terrace

*Below:* Ground floor of the grandstand

matches were abandoned in the 1960s, as were the segregated facilities.

A former heavyweight boxing champion and casino owner named John Morrissey developed Saratoga Race Course with William R. Travers, John R. Hunter, and Leonard W. Jerome as partners. Morrissey is considered to be the first owner of the racetrack. The *Republican & Sentinel* of July 8, 1864, describes in detail the new one-mile course and a grandstand with reception rooms, saloons, and halls on the lower floor, with a colonnade that ran the entire length (200 feet) of the building. Following Morrissey were various owners of the track from 1864 to 1902—all of whom were also casino owners. The last of the casino owners to own the track was Gottfried Walbaum, who built the grandstand and betting ring in 1891 and 1892, and then sold the track to a syndicate headed by W.C. Whitney in about 1900.

The noted event at Saratoga Race Course is the saddling of horses under the trees, and for nearly a century the public participated in this event. Before 1963 the paddock was a vast lawn where anybody could look at the horse. Each stable had a cluster of trees that served as an outdoor stall and exercise area where the horse was saddled before a race. Everybody convened in the paddock: the horse and groom came from the barn area, the jockey from the jockeys' quarters, the trainer and owner probably came from the clubhouse, and anybody else who was interested in observing the horses before placing a bet convened there. Although the paddock area is extremely large, it was once larger, having extended from the clubhouse across the drive into what is now used as a parking lot. The saddling is still done under the trees, but is now within a fenced area that largely excludes the public. The spectators now must view the horses from behind a fiberglass fence—any chance of a good look at the horse is gone. However, the public seems willing to accept this restricted viewing and limited access. The best view is reserved for television. In 1986 the track installed a television-camera stand in the center of the walking circle. It is covered by a canopy designed so that the camera can make a 360-degree turn.

The camera canopy is made of modern materials fashioned to look old, and this technique typifies the favored method of construction at Saratoga. The Red Spring is a pavilion that was moved from another location to the present spot and renamed the "Big" Red Spring. But during the long August days it is invigorating to drink the pavilion's tepid mineral water, regardless of its inauthenticity. The infield gazebo, which was designed by Mark Costello in the 1970s as a temporary bandstand for the backyard, is also an example of new materials put to an unusual use. Copper balls from toilet tanks and chipboard bases for funeral wreaths form its Victorian decoration, and its aluminum roof is painted to look like copper. Moving it to the infield and away from close scrutiny has improved its success as a building—its proportions are lovely and it has become an accepted piece of landscape architecture that makes as much sense as the aluminum canoe on the nearby lake. The jockeys' quarters is a reassembled house from the 1970s: the gable is a new construction, the posts were taken from an earlier building (which had been the polo clubhouse and was adapted to jockeys' quarters and offices in 1902), and the wrought-iron fence was brought from the parking area. Indeed, the jockeys' quarters, usually completely out of view, out of

*Above*: Approach to the grandstand from the backyard

*Below*: Back of the grandstand

*Overleaf*: The old clubhouse entrance

earshot, and off-limits at most racetracks, is located in the middle of the backyard. As Costello points out: "Now the jockeys' quarters is an event the public can watch. People can observe them play horseshoes and talk, and young girls can solicit autographs. It is a way for families to participate."

Costello traces the change at Saratoga to the era before off-track betting was introduced, when the crowds averaged 60,000 daily and 82,000 on the biggest race days. The grandstand could not possibly hold such a crowd, and although the infield had previously been used to relieve congestion, Costello says that "we could never count on it as a predictable solution because we could not protect people in the infield from sudden summer rains. People would cross the track while horses were running, and lose their shoes. The expansion of the grandstand, which currently seats 8,000, made it possible to comfortably hold 20,000 people in the grandstand area. This meant that 30,000 to 60,000 people, depending on the day, had to fit into the backyard. Apparently there were too many people too close to the horses. Ten acres were added by paring away at the paddock, so that the "expansion program of the backyard along with insurance problems caused elimination of saddling under the trees where the public could participate. Now all the saddling is done under the trees but in the fenced area," says Costello. Furthermore, he notes a change in general attitude. "In an effort to accommodate the grandstand patron, [we] set up all kinds of souvenir stands and concession stands. Now it is like a carnival in the backyard [whereas] in the past it was strictly a horseracing activity." But he admits that the formula works and that all the books, painted plates, T-shirts, food, beer, Saratoga sunrises, and lemonade provide entertainment. "It's a happening when you come here, but at Aqueduct and Belmont it tends to be business—the horse itself and betting." By the 1970s attendance had declined due to simulcasting, and although the attendance at Saratoga still increases annually, it is inconceivable that 80,000 people would attend. A handful of people behind a fiberglass fence and a general public with souvenirs of horses unfortunately forms the new Saratoga.

In early August, over a period of one or two days, 2,000 horses are shipped to Saratoga from all over the country, somewhat like children arriving at summer camp with all their paraphernalia. They are placed in stables that are located all over the racetrack. During the first fifty years the stable owners erected their own barns, building them in their favorite spots. A group of barns located at the far turn is known as Millionaire's Row, a name reflecting the wealth of the owners. Another group of stables, Clare Court, is located on the backstretch across from the grandstand, and the barns at Oklahoma Track are located across Union Avenue. There are eighty-six barns in all, spread over 350 acres. Horses cross the highway at Union Avenue on their way to the paddock, stopping traffic and adding to the pageantry of the racing season. After the New York Racing Association became the owner of the track in 1955, private ownership of the barns was eliminated. Any owner or stable can now apply for stall space for the racing season; the 2,000 stalls are free of charge and are in much demand. The stable area at Oklahoma Track is older than Saratoga Race Course. Horse Haven is a compound situated on a slightly raised oval site of large barns with Greek

*Above*: Easy Goer entering the track

*Below*: Horses going to the paddock

*Above*: The winner's circle

*Below*: The clubhouse

*Right*: The saddling shed

*Above*: The backyard through the balcony railing

*Below*: Decorative ironwork on the clubhouse balcony

Revival detailing and board-and-batten stables; all are painted gray, have slate roofs, and are located amid tall pines. Although there is no written documentation regarding the origin of the name of Oklahoma Track, it is generally thought that it refers to its distant location, for it was named at a time when Oklahoma seemed as remote as Mars.

The infield plantings and lake date from around 1902; a row of hydrangea bushes and a curve of canna lilies suggest a Victorian garden. The infield also contains a pair of joined poles that form an information tower, where, by a rope-and-pulley system, a signboard is hoisted with such information as jockey and horse changes. (A twin to this tower was installed recently to add symmetry, although symmetry was hardly necessary, and, since a tote board already gives this information such a tower is no longer useful.) The infield lake is famous for its canoe—a romantic reference to an Indian maiden. In line with the finishing post and wire, which forms a tangible connection between the infield and the grandstand, is the winner's circle. It lies at the base of the official's tower and is a modest rectangle

*Above:* Decorative ironwork of horses racing by steward's stand

enclosed by a wrought-iron fence. The tiny pavilion is covered with a canvas awning to protect the scales from the weather. The other, almost obsolete, winner's circle used here is a traditional circle drawn in the dirt with a mixture of chalk and flour.

Since Saratoga is the oldest track in America, it is important to note its influence on all other tracks. In terms of design, nearly all the other American Thoroughbred tracks repeat something of Saratoga.

*Above*: The early saddling shed, now enclosed

*Above and below*: The paddock

*Above*: Infield

*Above*: The infield lake and gazebo

*Above*: Barn area at Horse Haven

*Above*: Barn near Oklahoma Track

*Overleaf*: The boxes

# GLOSSARY

The entries below marked with a "CS" are contributions by Cathy Schenck, Librarian, Keeneland Race Course.

ADDED MONEY  Money added by the racing association to stakes fees paid by subscribers to form the total purse for a stakes race. (CS)

ALLOWANCE RACE  A race in which published conditions stipulate weight allowances according to previous purse earnings and/or number or type of wins. (CS)

APRON  The paved strip between the front of the grandstand and the track.

BACKSTRETCH  The straight part of the racing oval between the two turns at the back of the track. The straightaway in front of the grandstand from the turn to the finish line is the homestretch.

BETTING RING  That portion of the track where wagers are made, more common before the introduction of parimutuel betting. (CS)

BLOODLINE  The genealogy of a Thoroughbred horse.

BOOKMAKER  A person who quotes odds on various horses, receives bets on those horses, and pays the winning bets. (CS)

BREEDER  The owner of the dam of a horse at the time the horse was foaled. (CS)

BREEDERS' CUP  A championship series of million-dollar races to determine which is the best horse and to stimulate public interest in racing. The Breeders' Cup has been held each fall since 1983 and offers seven races for all age, sex, and distance divisions: Sprint, ¾ mile for three-year-olds and up; Juvenile Fillies, 1¹⁄₁₆ miles for two-year-old fillies; Distaff, 1⅛ miles for fillies and mares three years old and up; Two-Mile, 1 mile (turf) for three-year-olds and up; Juvenile, ¹⁄₁₆ mile for two-year-old colts and geldings; Turf, 1½ miles for three-year-olds and up; and Classic, 1¼ miles for three-year-olds and up. The idea was conceived by John R. Gaines, founder of Gainesway Farm in Lexington, Kentucky, to provide an international focal point at the end of each racing season. It is held at host racetracks and has initiated major capital improvements at each of the selected tracks.

CALLER  The person who calls out the running positions of the horses during a race.

CHUTE  An extra length of track added to provide a long straight run from the starting gate to the first turn.

CLAIMING RACE  A race in which all horses are entered for a specific price and can be purchased by another owner who has started a horse at the current meeting. Claiming races are used to provide competition between horses of similar value or racing records. (CS)

CLASSIC RACES  A series of races for three-year-old horses that are of set distances and run on the same days every year. The best American examples are the Kentucky Derby, 1¼ miles, run on the first Saturday in May; the Preakness, 1³⁄₁₆ miles, run two weeks later; and the Belmont Stakes, 1½ miles, run three weeks after the Preakness, in June.

CLERK OF SCALES  The official who weighs the jockeys before and after each race to ensure that proper weight was carried. (CS)

CLOCKER  A person who times the speed of a horse during workouts. Most clockers work for the *Daily Racing Form*, where the times of workouts are published for the racing public. (CS)

CLUBHOUSE  Originally a separate building, the clubhouse is now a section of the main racetrack building reserved for special ticket holders; it usually has the best seats and always contains a restaurant and bar.

CLUBHOUSE TURN  The first bend of the track, at the point where the clubhouse is usually situated.

COLOR  The official colors of Thoroughbreds registered with the Jockey Club are bay, brown, chestnut, black, gray, and roan, although 90 percent are bay, brown, and chestnut. (CS)

COLOR ROOM  The room used to store the jackets called silks or colors, worn by the jockeys for the various owners. The jackets are usually hung from metal hooks either around the ceiling of the room, as at Oaklawn, or on racks, as at Keeneland. They are managed by the silks man who makes them available to the jockeys' valets, who dress the jockeys before each race.

COLORS  Racing silks, jacket, and cap worn by jockeys to denote ownership of a horse. First introduced in England around 1762 when nineteen men registered owners' colors with the Jockey Club. Originally made from silk or satin. (CS)

COURSE  The racing strip, also called the track in America. It can refer to either a dirt or turf course, or be the name of the racetrack itself. The most stalwart of the old American racing tracks bear this name, as in Keeneland Race Course. Written as one word in the European manner, "racecourse" connotes an international facility, as in the newly renamed Arlington International Racecourse in Chicago. The racetracks that have always been presented as recreational facilities tend to be called parks, such as Oaklawn Park, Santa Anita Park, and Monmouth Park, although there are exceptions.

DAILY RACING FORM  The racing newspaper, started in Chicago in

1894 by Frank Brunell, that gives racing charts and past performances of race horses. The *Daily Racing Form* also publishes the times of workouts for the racing public. (CS)

FINISH LINE  A wire stretched above the track designating the finish; it is attached to a post with a mirror. It is sometimes called the wire. The term "wire to wire" is used when a horse takes the lead from the start of the race and holds this position until the finish.

GAP  The horse path leading from the paddock to the track, forming the entrance to the track. The term probably derived from the gap between the grandstand and the clubhouse in early racetracks.

GRADED STAKES RACE  A nonrestricted race with added money of $50,000 or more. Graded race status is conferred by the Thoroughbred Owners and Breeders Association (TOBA) North American Graded Stakes Committee. (CS)

According to Trevor Denmam, race commentator at Santa Anita: "Graded races were devised as an easy reference to grade the quality of stakes races across the country and internationally. The grading is based upon the performances of the field of horses that run in the stakes race and on the performances of those horses in subsequent races; the statistics are compiled to reflect the running history for about five years. The selection panel, composed of a team of racing secretaries from Florida, New York, and California, compiles these statistics and looks at the results retrospectively, determining Grades I, II, and III. For example, if the horses in the field of a particular stakes race went on to win other races, the stakes race would be considered a 'productive race' and could be upgraded from II to I. This method has been employed since about 1971 and is based entirely on cold facts."

GRANDSTAND  The main building of the racetrack, used primarily for spectators to view and place bets on the races.

HANDICAP  A race in which compensations are given to different horses according to their experience or ability to equalize the chances of winning. The criteria are past performances, weight carried, track conditions, jockey, and distance of the race, among others. The *American Heritage Dictionary* states that the origin is from "hand in cap," a lottery game in which players held forfeits in a cap.

HANDICAP RACE  A race in which the weights to be carried by the horses are assigned by the racing secretary according to the merits and performances of the horses entered. (CS)

HOT WALKER  A person who walks a horse after a workout to cool the horse down.

INFIELD  The part of the track surrounded by the racing oval. It is usually an open, landscaped area, sometimes containing a lake.

JOCKEY  A professional rider of race horses. (CS)

JOCKEY CLUB, THE  An organization started in 1894 that maintains the American Stud Book and approves Thoroughbred names and registry. Also the governing body responsible for the standardization of the rules of racing. (CS)

JOCKEYS' QUARTERS  A group of rooms for jockeys, usually consisting of a steam room, a room where the jockey dresses, and another room where the jockey either relaxes or waits for the races he is to ride.

MAIDEN RACE  A race for a horse that has not yet won any races. (CS)

OWNER  Any person who holds, in whole or in part, any right, title, or interest in a horse. (CS)

PADDOCK  Where the horses are saddled and kept before proceeding to the track. In the paddock the owner has his last moment with the jockey and trainer, and the patrons are able to see the horses for the first and only time of the day before making a swift appraisal of their condition and temperament in order to place a bet.

PADDOCK JUDGE  The official in charge of all activities in the saddling paddock before each race. (CS)

PARIMUTUELS  1. A system of betting in which the total amount bet on a particular race, less the track's percentage, is divided by the number of winning tickets, thus giving the price each winning ticket pays. This system originated in France and was first introduced in the United States in the 1870s. 2. The machine that records bets placed under this system. The *American Heritage Dictionary* traces the word to the French *parier*, to make equal, but in the American racing world it is generally thought that the word is derived from the city of Paris.

PATROL JUDGES  Officials who observe the progress of a race from various vantage points around the running strip. (CS)

PLACING JUDGES  Officials who determine the order of finish of a race. (CS)

POST  The starting gate.

POST PARADE  This occurs when the horses leave the gap and parade in front of the grandstand before proceeding to the starting gate.

POST POSITION  The horse's position in the starting gate, selected from a draw.

POST TIME  The designated time for the start of the race.

PURSE  The amount of money for which a race is run. The term originated from a custom in the late 1800s of hanging a silk purse containing the race money in front of the judges' stand. (CS)

RACE MEETING  The established number of racing days and fixed number of races that are held at each particular racetrack.

RACING COMMISSION  A commission designated in each state to regulate racing within that state.

RACING SECRETARY  The official responsible for writing the conditions for the races of a meeting. The conditions—purse money, claiming prize, weight, sex, and earnings—are published in a condition book which is distributed to trainers. (CS)

RAIL  The fence that separates the racing strips, as between the dirt track and the inner turf track, and both from the infield. There is an inside rail, where the horses run, and an outside rail, which acts as a barrier.

RECEIVING BARN  A barn that houses horses shipped in for a certain race. It is sometimes called an isolation barn or, in the case of international horses, a quarantine barn.

SILKS  The name of the shirt worn by the jockey identifying the stable for which he is riding. (See COLORS)

STABLE  The building where horses are housed. It also refers to a group of horses under an ownership.

STAKES RACE  Any race in which entries are made at least seventy-two hours in advance and which requires payment of subscription, entry, and starting fees by the owners. (CS)

STARTER  The official who gives the signal for the horses to begin a race. (CS)

STARTING GATE  A metal structure with partitions for horses which have gates on each side. The horses are loaded into the partitions for a few moments until the starter opens the gates in front of them, thus starting the race.

STEWARDS  Officials who supervise the conduct of a race meeting. They interpret and enforce the rules of racing, and their authority supersedes that of the racing association. (CS)

STRETCH  The straight portion of the racetrack between the final turn and the finish line.

STUD BOOK  The registry and record of the breeding of Thoroughbreds.

STUD FARM  A farm that houses stallions that are used for breeding.

THOROUGHBRED  A distinctive breed of horse tracing its genealogy back to horses registered in the English General Stud Book (1791), the American Stud Book (1896), the French Stud Book (1838), or a stud book of another country. (CS)

By 1700 the English had long been aware of the speed of Arabian horses; they had some horses that were spoils of war and started breeding them to English mares. Racing and breeding records were private until the eighteenth century, when several volumes were compiled. The first was a record of all English races valued ten pounds or more, published in 1727; this was continued under the name *Sporting Calendar* with the addition of pedigrees in 1743. It soon became clear that the horses that performed well could be traced back to Eastern, Arab, Barbary, or Turk descent. The first English stud book, titled the *General Stud Book*, was published in 1791 and was a listing of horses with good racing performances and their pedigrees. This was not a book about bloodlines per se, but a book about racing bloodlines. This particular book is recognized as documenting the beginning of a new breed of horse, the Thoroughbred—a racing horse that combined mostly Arab, Barbary, or Turkish blood with English stamina and strength. Originally the book merely listed horses that raced and proved to be winning horses. Now the *General Stud Book* has become the racing bible because only horses with bloodlines that can be traced back to it can be entered in Thoroughbred races. Thoroughbreds are horses descended from ancestors bred and trained for racing; the best among them are selected to breed in order to improve and carry on the line. Americans developed the sport concurrently with the English and French.

THOROUGHBRED INDUSTRY  The business of breeding and racing Thoroughbred horses. (CS)

TIMER  The official who records the length of time in which a race is run. (CS)

TOTE BOARD  An electronic panel that displays such information as post time and time of day. Recently, the tote board has included digital pictures of the leading horses from the starting gate to the $\frac{1}{8}$-mile pole.

TRAINER  The person responsible for the proper care, health, condition, and safety of horses in his charge. (CS)

TRUE RACES  Races with as little as possible left to chance.

WORKOUT  A training exercise during which the horse is timed for speed over a specified distance. (CS)

TURF COURSE  A grass racing strip.

VALET  The person who attends to the jockey, keeps equipment in order, acts as a dresser, and helps saddle the horse in the paddock.

WALKING RING  The circular or oval path in the paddock area where horses and jockeys parade before entering the horse path leading to the track. This is for the benefit of people in the paddock area who want to see the horse and rider before placing a bet. The post parade takes place for the benefit of those in the grandstand.

WHIP  The jockey's crop or stick.

WINDOWS  The site where bets are placed at a racetrack.

WINNER'S CIRCLE  A small area where the jockey brings the horse after winning a race, to weigh in, meet with the owner or trainer, and be photographed.

# SELECTED BIBLIOGRAPHY

## BOOKS

Allison, William. *The British Thoroughbred Horse: His history and breeding together with an exposition of the figure system.* London: Richards, 1901.

Anderson, James Douglas. *Making the American Thoroughbred Especially in Tennessee 1800–1845.* Norwood, Mass.: Plimpton Press, 1916.

Battell, Joseph. *American Stallion Register including all stallions prominent in the breeding of the American roadster, trotter, and pacer from the earliest records to 1902.* Middlebury, Vt.: American Publishing Co., 1909–36.

Becker, Friedrich. *The Breed of the Racehorse: Its Developments and Transformations.* London: British Bloodstock Agency, 1936.

Bobinski, Kazimierz. *Family Tables of Racehorses.* London: Lt. Col. Stefan Count Zamoyski, 1953.

Bolus, Jim. *Run for the Roses: 100 Years at the Kentucky Derby.* New York: Hawthorn Books, 1974.

Bowmar, Daniel M. *Giants of the Turf: The Alexanders, The Belmonts, James R. Keene, The Whitneys.* Lexington, Ky.: The Blood-Horse, 1960.

Bruce, Sanders D. *The American Stud Book: Containing full pedigrees of all imported Thoroughbred stallions and mares, with their produce, including the Arabs, Barbs, and Spanish horses.* New York: S. D. Bruce, 1873.

Burch, Preston Morris. *Training Thoroughbred Horses.* Lexington, Ky.: The Blood-Horse, 1953.

Cook, Theodore Andrea. *A History of the English Turf.* Three Volumes. London: H. Virtue and Co., 1901–1904.

Culver, Francis B. *Blooded Horses of Colonial Days.* Baltimore: F. B. Culver, 1922.

Daingerfield, Keene. Training for Fun and Profit—Maybe. Lexington, Ky.: Thoroughbred Record, 1942.

Harrison, Fairfax. *The Background of the American Stud Book.* Richmond, Va.: Old Dominion Press, 1933.

———. *The Belair Stud 1747–1761.* Richmond, Va.: Old Dominion Press, 1929.

———. *Early American Turf Stock 1730–1830.* Richmond, Va.: Old Dominion Press, 1934.

———. *The Equine F.F.Vs.: A study of the evidence for the English horses imported into Virginia before the Revolution.* Richmond, Va.: Old Dominion Press, 1934.

———. *The John's Island Stud 1750–1788.* Richmond, Va.: Old Dominion Press, 1931.

*The Roanoke Stud 1795–1833.* Richmond, Va.: Old Dominion Press, 1930.

Hayes, Matthew Horace. *Points of the Horse: A Treatise on the Conformation, Movements, Breeds, and Evolution of the Horse.* London: Hurst, 1904.

———. *Veterinary Notes for Horse Owners: An Illustrated Manual of Horse Medicine and Surgery.* New York: Prentice Hall Press, 1987.

Herbert, Ivor. *Horse Racing: The Complete Guide to the World of the Turf.* New York: St. Martin's Press, 1981.

Hervey, John. *Racing in America 1665–1865.* New York: The Jockey Club, 1944.

———. *Racing in America 1922–1936.* New York: The Jockey Club, 1937.

Hewitt, Abram S. *The Great Breeders and Their Methods.* Lexington, Ky.: Thoroughbred Publishers, 1982.

———. *Sire Lines.* Lexington, Ky.: Thoroughbred Owners and Breeders Association, 1977.

Hildreth, Samuel C. *The Spell of the Turf: The Story of American Racing.* Philadelphia: Lippincott, 1926.

Hislop, John. *Breeding for Racing.* London: Secker, 1976.

Hollingsworth, Kent. *The Great Ones.* Lexington, Ky.: The Blood-Horse, 1970.

Hore, John Philip. *The History of Newmarket and the Annals of the Turf.* London: A. H. Baily and Co., 1886.

Irving, John Beaufain. *The South Carolina Jockey Club.* Charleston, S.C.: Russell & Jones, 1857.

Kelley, Robert F. *Racing in America 1937–1959.* New York: The Jockey Club, 1960.

Lehndorff, Georg Hermann. *Horse Breeding Recollections.* London: H. Cox, 1883.

Leicester, Sir Charles. *Bloodstock Breeding.* Revised by Howard Wright. London: J. A. Allen, 1983.

McLean, Ken. *Quest for a Classic Winner: Pedigree Patterns of the Racehorse.* Lexington, Ky.: K. A. and C. J. McLean, 1987.

O'Conor, John Lawrence. *Notes on the Thoroughbred from Kentucky Newspapers.* Lexington, Ky.: Transylvania Printing Co., 1927.

Palmer, Joseph Hill. *Names in Pedigrees.* Lexington, Ky.: The Blood–Horse, 1939.

———. *This Was Racing.* New York: Barnes, 1953.

Prior, C. M. *Early Records of the Thoroughbred Horse: Containing Reproductions of some Original Stud-Books and other papers of the Eighteenth Century.* London: Sportsman, 1924.

Ridgeway, Sir William. *The Origin and Influence of the Thoroughbred Horse.* Cambridge: University Press, 1905.

Robertson, William H. P. *The History of Thoroughbred Racing In America.* Englewood Cliffs, N.J.: Prentice-Hall 1964.

Rudy, William H. *Racing in America 1960–1979.* New York: The Stinehour Press, 1980.

Stubbs, George. *The Anatomy of the Horse.* London: J. Purser, 1766.

Tesio, Federico. *Breeding the Racehorse.* London: Allen, 1958.

Ulbrich, Richard. *The Great Stallion Book.* Hobart, Australia: Libra Books, 1986.

Varola, Franco. *The Functional Development of the Thoroughbred.* London: Allen, 1980.

———. *Typology of the Racehorse.* London: Allen, 1974.

Vosburgh, Walter Spencer. *Racing in America 1866–1922.* New York: The Jockey Club, 1922.

Wall, John Furman. *Thoroughbred Bloodlines: An Elementary Study.* Baltimore: Monumental Printing Co., 1939.

Weeks, Lyman Horace. *The American Turf: An Historical Account of Racing in the United States with Biographical Sketches of Turf Celebrities.* New York: Historical Co., 1898.

## ANNUALS

*American Race Horses.* New York: Sagamore Press, 1936–63. A review of the breeding and the performances of the outstanding Thoroughbreds of the year.

*American Racing Manual.* Chicago: Daily Racing Form Publishing Co., 1906–present.

*American Stud Book.* New York: The Jockey Club, 1898–present. Published every four years. Supplement published annually.

*Bloodstock Breeders Review.* London: British Bloodstock Agency, 1912–81. An illustrated annual devoted to the British Thoroughbred.

*General Stud Book.* London: Weatherby & Sons, 1791–present.

*Goodwin's Annual Official Turf Guide.* New York: Goodwin Bros., 1883–1908.

*Krik's Guide to the Turf: Record of Races Run in the United States.* New York: Crickmore, 1877–1882.

*Racing Calendar.* London: Weatherby & Sons, 1773–1971. Published for The Jockey Club.

*Stud Book Français.* Paris: L'Institut du Cheval, 1839–present.

*Timeform.* London: Portway, 1944–present.

## PERIODICALS

*American Turf Register and Sporting Magazine.* Baltimore and New York: 1829–1844. Monthly.

*The Blood-Horse.* Lexington, Ky.: 1929–present. Weekly.

*Charts of American Racing.* Chicago: 1894–present. Monthly.

*Spirit of the Times: A Chronicle of the Turf.* New York: 1831–1861. Weekly.

*Thoroughbred Record.* Lexington, Ky.: 1875–1990. Weekly.

*Turf, Field and Farm.* New York: 1865–1902. Weekly.

# INDEX